ASTRONOMY

igloo

First published in 2007
This edition published in 2011
by Igloo Books Ltd
Cottage Farm,
Sywell,
NN6 0BJ

www.igloo-books.com

Copyright © 2007 Igloo Books Ltd

Cataloguing in Publication Data information
2 4 6 8 10 9 7 5 3 1

B044 0811

ISBN: 978-0-85780-123-4

Printed in China

Author: Paul Sutherland

Front Cover Image - Getty Images,
All other images: NASA, ESO, ESA, SOHO, Paul Sutherland,
Shutterstock.com, istock.com, Clipart.com
Star maps created in conjunction with Stellarium software
(www.stellarium.org)/American Association of Variable Star
Observers
American Association of Amateur Astronomers, Anthony Ayiomamitis, '
Neil Bone, Fred Bruenjes, Celestron, Sebastian Deiries, Colin Ebdon,
Yoji Hirose,David Graham, Peter Grego, Yoko Kikuta
R. Ligustri and Herman Mikuz, Meade Instruments, Optical Vision
Dave Pearson, Philipp Salzgeber, Juergen Schmoll
Nik Szymanek, Dave Tyler, David Strange, Leo Stachowicz

CONTENTS

INTRODUCTION

We on planet Earth are infinitesimally tiny specks on the cosmic stage. But, by looking out, we can marvel at the nature of the universe and appreciate the wonders of the heavens for ourselves.

The study of everything beyond the Earth is called astronomy. This is clearly an enormous subject, but it is also makes for a fascinating hobby. There is so much out there, so much to see. To lose yourself in space is a great antidote to the stresses of everyday life.

Astronomers have long shed the image of old men with long white beards. And you don't need a brain the size of a planet and a bottomless wallet to take up stargazing.

There is so much to discover by watching our sky. There are constellations to identify and planets to spot. To do this all that is required is enthusiasm to learn about the vast universe that surrounds us.

This book will help you in your exploration of the universe by explaining the basics of what it is all about, in plain English. It will also show how you can become an astronomer, with beginners' guides on taking up different areas of stargazing.

Above all, we hope to show that astronomy is much more than complex research. As a hobby, it's tremendous fun!

NATURE OF THE HEAVENS

Our view of the sky is like looking out from the inside of a goldfish bowl.

Our view of the sky is not fixed. It changes as time passes, from hour to hour and day to day. Stars and planets are visible at some times but absent at others. To understand why, we need to appreciate a few basic concepts. First, the Earth is a ball in space, surrounded by all the objects in the universe. From any one point on its surface, we can look up and see around half of the sky at a time. But the Earth is also rotating.

As the Earth turns, the sky seems to wheel in the opposite direction. The most obvious indicator of this to us is the Sun, which we see rising, crossing the sky and setting each day. We may not have noticed it, but all the other objects such as stars, rotate across the sky in a similar way.

It's as if they are all fixed to a spinning goldfish bowl that we are observing from the inside. Of course, it is we who are spinning and not the bowl, but we get the impression that it is turning rather than us.

Astronomers term this virtual goldfish bowl the Celestial Sphere. It appears to rotate around two Celestial Poles directly above the Earth's own North and South Poles.

An imaginary grid can be drawn on this sphere, matching the longitude and latitude grid that was created for the Earth.

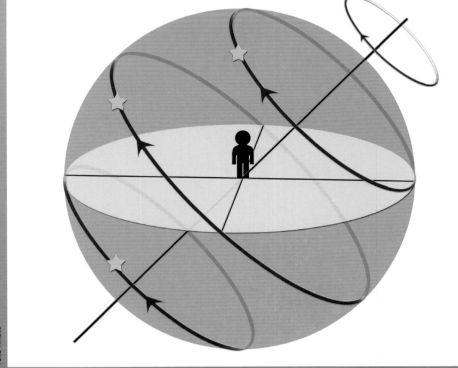

Yoko Kikuta

An observer at a mid-northern latitude sees stars rise, cross the sky and set. But stars close to the North Celestial Pole always stay above the horizon. Others around the South Celestial Pole never rise at all.

Leaving a camera's shutter open for many minutes or even hours shows clearly how circumpolar stars revolve around the celestial pole as the Earth rotates.

Lines joining the two Celestial Poles — the equivalent of longitude — are termed Right Ascension and are measured in hours and minutes. Lines parallel to the Equator, similar to our lines of latitude, are termed Declination and are measured in degrees. The line at 0 degrees running directly above the Equator is called the Celestial Equator. Positions north of it take positive values up to +90 degrees at the North Celestial Pole. Points south of the Equator count down to -90 degrees at the South Celestial Pole.

Although the whole sky appears to rotate around an axis, not all stars rise and set (unless you live on the Equator). Our location determines which stars set and which do not.

From the North or South Pole, all the stars appear to move parallel to the horizon. From the Equator, they all appear to rise vertically from the horizon, pass over the sky and sink below the opposite horizon.

If you are at a spot somewhere between the North Pole and the Equator, the North Celestial Pole will appear to lie in the sky at an altitude equal to your own latitude. Stars close to the North Celestial Pole will never set. Conversely, the South Celestial Pole will always lie below your horizon and stars close to that will never rise at all. The diagram on page 6 shows this. The situation is reversed in the southern hemisphere.

The entire Celestial Sphere appears to rotate in a little under 24 hours, with everything moving from West to East.
Each star will make a complete journey around it and return to its original point in exactly 23 hours 56 minutes, which is the time it takes the Earth to rotate on its axis. This is called the Sidereal Period. But we all know that the day is actually 24 hours long, so where do the extra four minutes fit in?

The answer is found in the Earth's journey around the Sun in its orbit. This year-long trip makes the Sun appear to move from day to day against the starry background. It is highest in the sky at local noon but takes 24 hours to reach its highest point the following day.

Before the invention of mechanical clocks and watches, man invented sundials which used the moving shadow cast by the Sun's daily motion across the sky to tell the time.

The other planets can be seen to move from night to night against the starry background in their orbits around the Sun. But the planets outside the Earth's orbit appear to backtrack, creating little loops in the sky, for a period of time every year.

Of course, they don't really change direction. The effect is similar to when you are in a car that overtakes a slower vehicle on the motorway. The other car appears to move backwards against the background. When we overtake the more distant planets, the same thing happens. This is called retrograde motion.

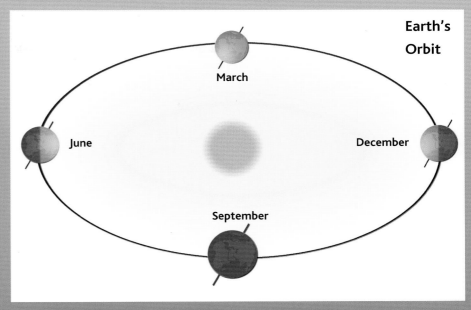

Earth's Orbit

March

June

December

September

The Earth's axis is tilted to the plane of its orbit around the Sun, giving rise to the seasons. The northern hemisphere is tilted towards the Sun in June, the time of its summer, but the position is reversed six months later when the southern hemisphere enjoys more sunshine.

Yoko Kikuta

The path that the Sun seems to follow against the sky is skewed against the lines of Declination that we encountered earlier. This happens because the Earth's polar axis is tilted by 23.5 degrees to the plane of its orbit around the Sun.

This means that the northern hemisphere is tilted towards the Sun in June (northern summer) and the Sun climbs high in the sky at noon.

The South Pole is tilted towards the Sun in December, when the southern hemisphere enjoys summer and the Sun is high at noon there. The path along which the Sun appears to move against the Celestial Sphere is termed the Ecliptic. It runs through the

"Although the whole sky appears to rotate around an axis, not all stars rise and set."

constellations of the Zodiac and crosses the Celestial Equator at the Equinoxes in March and September.

Because the planets have orbits that are more or less level with the Earth's, they too appear to move through the Ecliptic. So too does the Moon.

THE SOLAR SYSTEM

The Solar System is made up of the Sun and its family of planets, plus the other natural objects that circle it, condensed from a spinning cloud of dust and gas created more than four and a half billion years ago.

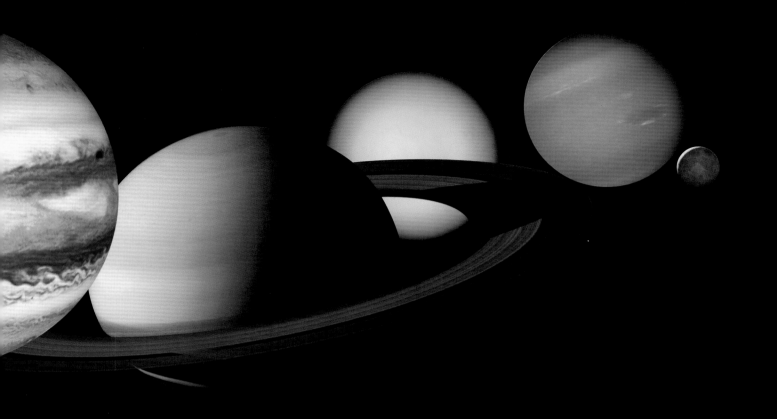

The Solar System includes the natural satellites or moons that orbit many of those planets, as well as countless smaller objects ranging from asteroids and comets down to tiny particles of dust.

In recent years we have discovered that our solar system is by no means unique. Telescopes on Earth and in space have detected planets in orbit around close to 200 stars, plus disks of dust where planets might be forming around others.

Astronomers today consider there to be eight main planets in our own solar system after Pluto was demoted in 2006 by a controversial gathering of the scientific powers that be, the International Astronomical Union.

The planets are named after Roman gods, continuing the tradition set by ancient man who were aware of the existence of all planets out as far as Saturn.

Earth is the third planet in order from the Sun. The two that lie between our parent star and us are Mercury and Venus. They are known as Inferior Planets because of their position relative to us. They are solid, rocky worlds like our own. The five major worlds that lie beyond Earth — Mars, Jupiter, Saturn, Uranus and Neptune — are known as Superior Planets. Again, that is due to their position rather than any decree as to their importance. All except Mars are giant balls of gas with no solid surface.

When viewed through a telescope, the inferior planets can be seen to change their appearance, like the Moon. They will resemble a not-quite-full moon when their orbit takes them further from Earth than the Sun, but as crescents as they close in between us and the Sun.

The point when Mercury or Venus lies between us and the Sun is called Inferior Conjunction and that where either lies at its furthest position beyond the Sun is described as Superior Conjunction.

Planets beyond the Earth are said to be in Conjunction when they lie on the far side of the Sun but at Opposition when the Earth lies between them and the Sun.

None except Mars — which resembles a nearly full moon at certain positions in its orbit — can show phases when viewed from Earth.

Any small telescope will bring into view the spectacular craters that have scarred the Moon's surface

A Full Moon shows the dark lunar seas, or maria, as well as bright material ejected from more recent impacts, though the lack of shadows renders most craters invisible.

THE MOON

Apart from the Sun, there is one other object that clearly dominates the skies — our celestial partner the Moon.

The Moon may be pretty insignificant on the grand scale of the cosmos, with a diameter of just 2,160 mi/3,475 km, but there is no astronomical body that shows itself to us in such detail.

The Moon is the Earth's only natural satellite and lies so close, at an average distance of just 240,000 mi/385,000 km, that we can enjoy wonderful views of its mountains, valleys and other formations. It is the only world other than our own that humans have visited and explored.

The naked eye is enough to detect some of the features on its surface, but any small telescope and even binoculars will bring into view the spectacular craters that have permanently scarred its surface.

Generally speaking, we only get to see the features on one side of the Moon because it keeps the same face toward us throughout its orbit. A gentle rocking, called Libration, does allow us to peek around at some of the far side, but more than 40 percent of the lunar surface remains permanently out of view from Earth.

The side of the Moon that we can see offers a wealth of features to keep backyard observers

> "The lunar landscape has barely changed over millions of years. But the features may take on a different appearance from night to night."

happy for a lifetime, though there is not an awful lot going on there because the Moon is basically a sterile rock devoid of any of the weather or other events that make many of the planets so interesting.

This means that the lunar landscape has barely changed over millions of years. For an observer, however, the features may put on a different appearance from night to night, and even hour to hour, as the angle of sunlight on them varies.

The Moon has no light of its own and shines purely because of reflected sunlight. As the

Moon travels in its orbit around the Earth, it shows different phases. To be strictly accurate, the two worlds rotate around one point marking their center of gravity, but it lies beneath the Earth's surface. Parts of the Moon move from darkness into daylight as the Sun rises over the local lunar horizon. This "daytime" period lasts for two weeks for any one spot on the Moon before the Sun sinks below the horizon again and the area is plunged into two weeks of gloom.

This darkness comes suddenly. There can be no twilight without any atmosphere. Temperatures plummet from more than 212°F/100°C to less than -275°F/-170°C. Inside some craters near the lunar poles are shadows that the Sun never reaches. Space scientists speculate that there may be ice buried in these permanently dark areas from cometary impacts long ago.

We see the phases change from a fine crescent in the evening sky through a half phase, then gibbous (as the waxing and waning are known), until Full Moon when the whole face presented to us is lit up. The process then reverses as the Moon continues its orbit and wanes back to a crescent in the morning sky. For a few days, the Moon becomes invisible as it lies in the same general

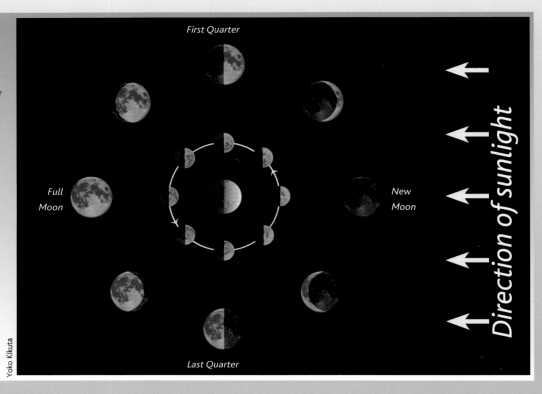

The Moon, which always keeps the same face towards the Earth, produces no light of its own. As it makes its month-long orbit, half of its surface is always illuminated by the Sun. The diagram shows how the changing phase of the Moon appears at different stages in this orbit.

First Quarter

Full Moon

New Moon

Last Quarter

Direction of sunlight

Yoko Kikuta

direction as the Sun. This is the time of New Moon, when the Sun's light falls entirely on its far side.

As the diagram above shows, half of the Moon is always in sunlight throughout this orbit. It's the changing position of the Moon relative to the Earth and the Sun that produces the phases. It can be a surprise to people to learn that the the Moon's orbit means it spends as much time in the daytime sky each month as it does the night.

When the Moon is showing as a fine crescent, it is often possible to make out the rest of it too. This phenomenon, dubbed "the new Moon in the old Moon's arms", is produced by sunlight reflecting off the Earth and illuminating the area of the Moon in shade.

The Moon is a lot less dense than the Earth, which rules out the idea that they might have formed as twin worlds. Instead, astronomers' favorite theory is that the Moon formed when another giant body collided with the Earth billions of years ago, throwing a vast quantity of our planet's outer layers into space. The material came together and slowly solidified into our satellite.

Until around a billion years ago, the Moon still had a hot interior. Major asteroid impacts would cause its outer crust to crack open, allowing molten lava to flood out. It formed the huge flat plains that we call the maria, or lunar seas. The seas are, of course, dry; there is no water.

Although there may still be a molten core,

the Moon is today largely a solid, inactive world. It is covered with a lunar soil, called regolith and around 30ft/10m deep, made of pulverized rocks and dust from billions of years of impacts. Occasional activity has been reported in some craters. Called Transient Lunar Phenomena, or TLPs, these may be signs of gas venting from the interior.

Recently, other genuine flashes have been detected in the part of the moon in shadow. These are thought to be due to tiny meteors exploding as they strike the Moon. They would burn up as shooting stars if they entered the Earth's atmosphere.

When observing the Moon, note that the best time is when the dividing line between its illuminated side and its dark side, called the terminator, is passing across the visible disk. At this time, lunar features nearby will cast strong shadows, showing them in dramatic relief. When the Moon is full, all the detail is lost because no shadows can be seen from Earth. The only features that stand out at this time are the maria and brilliant white rays crossing the surface that mark the ejected material from a few, relatively young impact craters. The Moon looks brilliant when full despite the fact that its rocks are actually very dark. The Moon has weak gravity, a sixth as strong as on Earth, which explains why the Apollo astronauts appeared to bounce along as they walked on its surface. But the pull is enough to cause the tides that raise and lower our seas every day. The Earth's own gravitational pull on the Moon is what locked its rotation over the years, so that the same side is always presented to us.

The Moon has an eccentric orbit, meaning that its distance from the Earth varies in distance by around 25,000mi/40,000 km. It appears larger in the sky when closest (called at perigee) than furthest (apogee), although the casual observer would find it difficult to notice the difference.

Robotic space probes have continued to study the Moon since the last Apollo astronauts walked on its surface in 1972. But NASA is working to send humans there again by 2020 and set up permanently manned colonies, as a first step to going to Mars.

NASA

The Moon is the only other world to have been visited by humans. Here the second man on the Moon, Buzz Aldrin, steps down the ladder from his lunar module to set foot on the lunar surface. Twelve astronauts walked on the Moon between 1969 and 1972 during the Apollo missions and NASA is making plans to go there again.

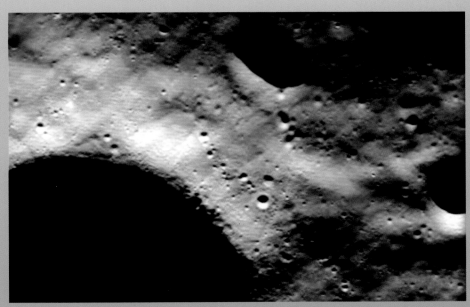

ESA

When astronauts return to the Moon, they may well stay in or near Shackleton crater. Scientists believe that ice may exist in craters like Shackleton which have areas permanently in shadow. If ice is there, it would make it easier to supply nearby moonbases with water.

THE SUN

The Sun is the great powerhouse at the center of the solar system around which its extensive family revolves.

It dominates our lives, its diameter of 864,950 mi/ 1,392,000 km is around 50 times greater than that of Jupiter, the largest planet in the Solar System. It is big enough to swallow up a million Earths.

On a cosmic scale, however, the Sun is not particularly special. It's an average star like the thousands of millions of others in our own Milky Way galaxy and the untold billions within the countless other galaxies in the universe.

Yet the Sun is special, indeed vital, to us because it provides the light and heat on which we all depend for survival. It does this not by burning like a fire, but by acting as a giant nuclear furnace, where atomic reactions occur on a vast scale.

The Sun does not burn like a fire but acts as a giant nuclear furnace where atomic reactions occur on a vast scale

These processes turn 7,000 million tons of hydrogen into helium every second, releasing the enormous amount of energy that makes the Sun shine.

What is incredible is that the Sun has already been converting hydrogen in this way for more than 4.5 billion years, and is expected to carry on doing so for a similar length of time.

Unlike other stars in the sky, the Sun is dazzlingly – indeed dangerously – bright. It also shows a sizeable face that astronomers can study in detail. Despite this, we know a lot less about our parent star than we would like, although a number of satellites are currently returning data that should improve our knowledge considerably.

The common perception that the Sun is yellow, is based on an illusion: it is really a white star. It is a ball of gas with no solid edge, so when we view its surface, called the photosphere, through filters, we are actually looking into a fog 300mi/500km deep. The temperature here is a staggering 9,900°F/5,500°C and photographs reveal the surface to be granulated like a pile of sugar: each cell is around 600 mi/1000 km across.

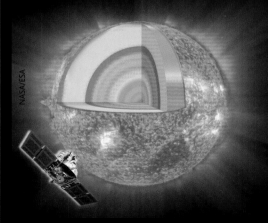

NASA/ESA

Scientists have been putting the Sun under close scrutiny, using satellites such as SOHO to monitor flares and solar storms which could threaten Earth.

This photosphere can be seen to be brighter towards the center than near the edges because we are looking at the hotter central regions of the Sun – it is thought that the temperature at the Sun's core may be as much as 60,000,000°F/15,000,000°C.

Notable features on the photosphere are the dark blotches that seem to appear suddenly and at random. These are called sunspots, a kind of solar acne formed from convection currents – regions 1,800°F/1,000°C or more cooler than the rest of the surface. They are surrounded by a lighter and warmer fringe that is termed the penumbra. Sunspots only look dark because they contrast with the solar disk's general brilliance. If one could be viewed in isolation, it would glow brightly.

Studies of these sunspots show that their appearance is not quite as random and unpredictable as one might think.

They are caused by disturbances in the Sun's magnetic field and are far more frequent at certain times than at others. Indeed, there is an 11-year cycle during which such solar activity grows and wanes.

Over that period, as well as changing their frequency, sunspots also tend to appear more at particular latitudes on the Sun's disk. This phenomenon is known as the Butterfly Effect due to the pattern created when spot occurrences are plotted on a graph.

Some sunspots are so big that they are several times the size of the Earth. Occasionally they are big enough to be seen with the naked eye – providing an appropriate solar filter is used. Ancient man was aware of sunspots and they were studied by the astronomer Galileo and others after the invention of the telescope.

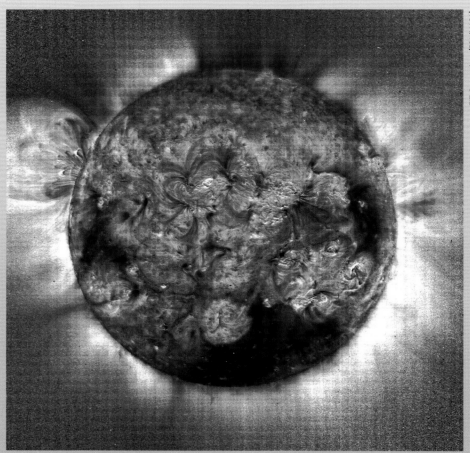

Hinode JAXA/NASA/PPARC

EIT Consortium (ESA/NASA)

The granulated surface of the Sun is clearly revealed in an image from a Japanese solar satellite called Hinode. This mottled pattern is caused by convection currents which carry hot gas from below the surface and then send it sinking again as it cools.

This dramatic image is a map of the Sun's corona indicating the different temperatures in its atmosphere. Brighter areas show the hotter regions of gas. It was made by the SOHO satellite on June 21, 2001, while a total solar eclipse was visible from southern Africa, allowing astronomers to compare observations from space with those made from the ground.

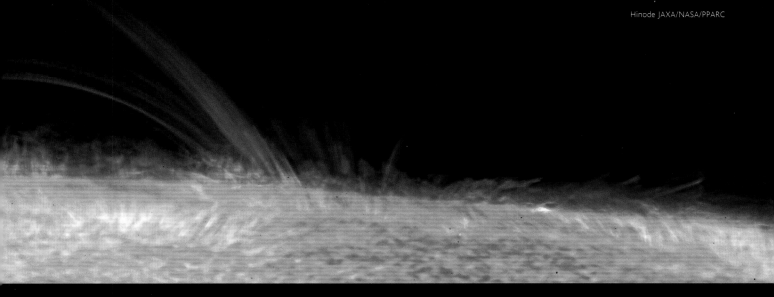

Hinode JAXA/NASA/PPARC

"Flame-like prominences revealed by specialist equipment are invisible in normal daylight. These eruptions can reach thousands of miles into space"

Long strands and wisps of gas stream from the thin layer of the Sun's atmosphere called the chromosphere .

These observations showed that the Sun spins on its axis and helped determine how long it takes to do so. Matters are complicated because the rotational period differs across the disk, but we now know that the Sun turns once every 26 days at the equator and between 30 and 36 days as you get nearer the poles.

Spots are not the only feature to be seen on the Sun. Faculae show like bright rivers of light and plages are other bright regions. Explosive events occasionally occur in the form of intense flares.

Flame-like prominences that specialist equipment reveals around the Sun's edge are invisible in normal daylight. These eruptions, which can form strands or loops reaching thousands of miles/kilometers into space, also

reveal themselves during a total eclipse of the Sun, when the solar atmosphere, called the chromosphere, also comes into view. Beyond the chromosphere is the corona, an extensive outer atmosphere, and beyond that streams the solar wind, a continual flow of high-speed gas.

Observatory satellites have detected another form of event called coronal mass ejections. These hurl electrically charged particles out into space and are the main cause of the aurora, the celestial light show that we call the northern and southern lights, when they hit the Earth's magnetic field.

Scientists have sent twin satellites called Stereo to watch for these ejections, from either side of the Earth, because they pose a real threat to satellite electronics, power grids and even the lives of astronauts.

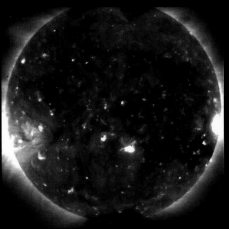

Hinode JAXA/NASA/PPARC

An X-ray view of the Sun from the Hinode satellite shows intensely bright regions where huge explosions of gas, powered by the Sun's magnetic field, are taking place. These coronal mass ejections hurl highly charged particles into space and can wreck satellite electronics.

OBSERVING THE SUN

The size and proximity of the Sun make it attractive for amateur astronomers. However, observing the Sun is highly dangerous unless you follow safety rules to the letter.

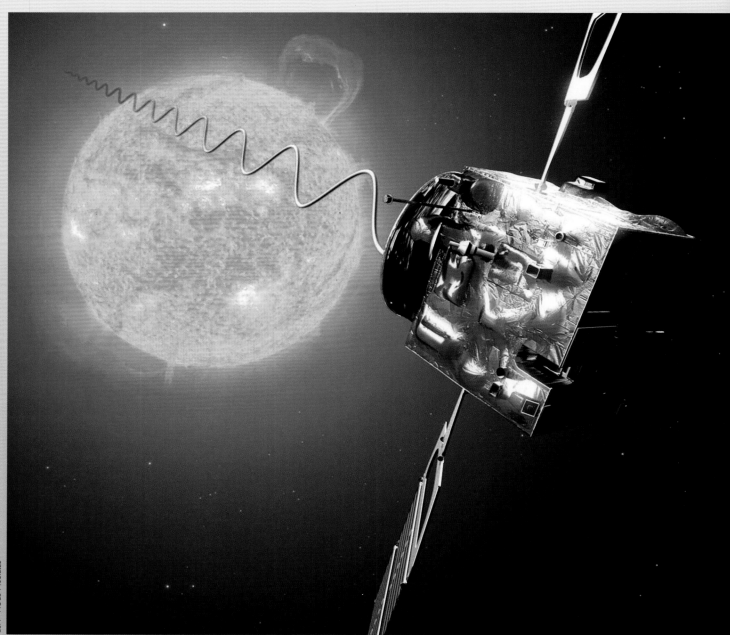

ESA - AOES Medialab

"Put the caps over the lenses of your telescope's finder, so that the sunlight does not pass through and burn you or set fire to clothing"

Traditionally, the safe way to observe the Sun has been to use a technique called projection. This entails aligning the telescope with the Sun so that its light shines down the tube, like any other object, but is then projected out of the eyepiece and onto a piece of card held a short distance away.

The Sun is so bright that this will produce a clear image. Focusing the telescope in the normal way allows the image to be sharp.

Putting the card in shadow will help the projected image to stand out more clearly. Some observers use black card instead of white, claiming this gives a much clearer image. Regular solar observers buy or build special projection screens to make life easier. This may be lined with a special graded disk to help to log the precise positions and sizes of any sunspots and so build a record of solar activity.

Some words of warning. Don't align the telescope by looking through it or along it. Use the instrument's shadow to tell when it is directed the right way. Also, put caps over the lenses of your telescope's finder, if you have one, so that sunlight does not pass through; it could burn you or set fire to clothing while you are observing. You should also check carefully that your telescope is

suitable for projecting the Sun. Many contain plastic rather than metal in the telescope tube and eyepieces, and this can melt under the magnified heat. Larger telescopes, particularly reflectors or SCTs, may need to have their apertures reduced, or "stopped down", to cut the amount of sunlight entering the tube. You may find that the cap that came with your scope has a smaller cap covering a hole in part of it for just this purpose.

In recent years, special filters have been produced, made in glass or of specialist coated film, that are placed over the main opening of the telescope to cut its light to a safe level for normal viewing. You can even buy miniature binoculars with filters built in purely for keeping an eye on the Sun. Only buy such filters from a reputable source and always check them for damage, such as holes or scratches.

Some telescopes used to come with a so-called solar filter for the eyepiece end of the telescope. If you have one, throw it away. They are not safe and can crack in the intense heat. Never try to make home-made filters, either. Colored film, dark photographic slides or CDs are not suitable. Even if they appear to filter the sunlight, they will let

An observer snaps the Sun through a compact telescope fitted with a dense protective filter to cut its powerful rays.

through invisible solar radiation which can permanently damage your eyes.

Special telescopes filter out most of the light spectrum, so the Sun's prominences may be viewed in hydrogen alpha light. These used to be prohibitively expensive because of the engineering involved, but today some mass-produced models are available at relatively affordable prices.

Left: Many sophisticated probes have been launched to investigate the Sun's mysteries – including the Venus Express shown here. But a properly prepared telescope can still provide fascinating insights.

ECLIPSES
OF THE SUN AND MOON

Eclipses are among the rarer events in the sky, and they are also among the most dramatic. There are two major types both of which involve alignments of the Sun, Moon and Earth.

SOLAR ECLIPSES

An eclipse of the Sun occurs when the Moon passes directly between us and the Sun. Technically, this is an occultation rather than an eclipse, which normally involves a body moving into shadow. A solar eclipse can only occur at New Moon.

By an amazing coincidence of nature, the Moon appears almost exactly the same size in the sky as the Sun, although this is solely because it lies so much closer to us.

It means that from parts of the Earth, the Moon can completely obliterate the Sun in broad daylight, temporarily turning day into night and revealing our home star's atmosphere, or corona, shining as a ghostly band around it, with perhaps a few prominences also in view.

An eclipse is the only time we get to view the corona from Earth. Its shape changes depending on the point the Sun has reached in its 11-year cycle of activity.

Around solar minimum, the glow stretches mainly from the equatorial regions and much less so towards its poles. Around solar maximum, the corona is more evenly spread all around the Sun's disk.

Because the Moon just covers the Sun, the area from which a total eclipse is visible is very small, perhaps 100mi/ 160km wide, on the Earth. This stretches into a lengthy eclipse track that can run for thousands of miles across continents as the Moon travels in its orbit and the Earth rotates below. But it means that from any one point on Earth, total eclipses are extremely rare. Partial eclipses which may be seen for hundreds of kilometers around, are more common. From these regions, the Moon only partly covers the Sun.

Key moments during an eclipse are called contacts. First contact, as the name suggests, is when the Moon limb first encroaches on the Sun.

Second contact is the moment when it completely covers the Sun and totality begins.

At third contact, the sun's light breaks through a lunar valley, producing the famous Diamond Ring Effect and marking the end of totality.

Fourth contact is when the Moon glides completely off the solar disk.

Only during the period of totality is it safe to look directly at the eclipse. Be sure to do so because it's an amazing spectacle. Look away, or use your eclipse specs again, the moment the Sun reappears.

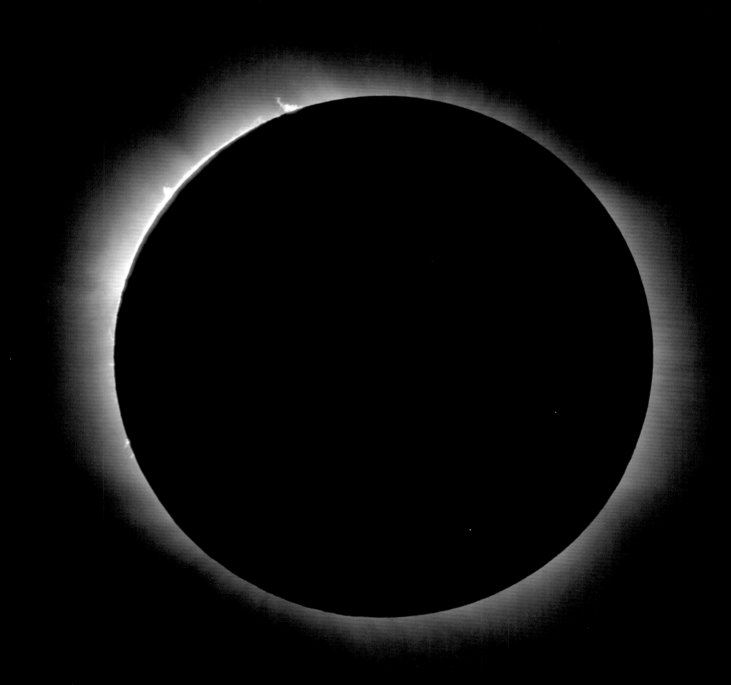

A total eclipse of the Sun is one of the most dramatic spectacles in nature and the only time when the solar atmosphere, or corona, can be viewed from the ground. Red flame-like prominences may also be spotted leaping from the edge of the Sun. Totality is the only time when it is safe to look at the Sun wth the naked eye.

A total lunar eclipse is a dramatic sight with the Moon turning red from sunlight scattered onto its surface through the Earth's atmosphere. It can take on a 3-D effect.

There is a further type of solar eclipse, called an annular eclipse. This occurs when the Moon is around its furthest distance from Earth and does not appear quite big enough in the sky to cover the Sun completely. When the two bodies align directly over a point on Earth, a ring of sunlight is left around the Moon's edge. This is the so-called Ring of Fire. Although they lack the subtleties of a total eclipse, annular eclipses are incredible to witness. You will need to protect your eyes throughout.

Solar eclipses do not happen every New Moon because the plane of the Moon's orbit is tilted by about five degrees to that of the Earth around the Sun, so that it normally passes above or below it. They occur at the points where the two orbits cross, called the nodes. Solar eclipses may be observed using the techniques described on pages 20 and 21. Alternatively, you can project a tiny image of the eclipse without a telescope by making a pinhole in a piece of card and allowing the Sun's light to shine through it on to a second piece of card.

LUNAR ECLIPSES

Eclipses of the Moon are true eclipses because they are caused when our natural satellite passes into the shadow of the Earth in space. They can only occur at Full Moon, but they do not occur at every Full Moon for the reasons of tilted orbits explained above. As it's the Moon's own appearance that changes during a lunar eclipse, the event is visible from any part of the world from which the Moon can be seen. You will therefore get the chance to see a lot more lunar eclipses than solar during your lifetime.

The Moon usually shines from reflected sunlight. The Sun also causes the Earth to cast a shadow, which is normally invisible in the sky. When the Moon drifts into the shadow, its light begins to fade.

At first the effect is only slight because the eclipse is penumbral – from the Moon,

the Earth would appear only partly to be obscuring the Sun. During some eclipses, the Moon only enters this twilight zone of the shadow. But when it passes through the central shadow, the Sun's light is completely blocked from falling on the Moon.

Or almost. During most total eclipses, the Moon remains visible, displaying a glow that ranges in color from orange to a deep red. This is because the Earth's atmosphere scatters sunlight, directing the longer reddish wavelengths on to the lunar disk and allowing it to remain in sight.

Astronomers watch in fascination to see how dark or bright a total lunar eclipse will be. It often gives a clue to the state of our atmosphere, because dark eclipses tend to occur in months following a major volcanic eruption that has ejected dust to high altitudes. Sometimes variations in the light can give the Moon a three-dimensional glow.

The total phase can last up nearly two hours, depending on how far into the center of the Earth's shadow the Moon has traveled. Passage through the entire shadow, including the penumbra, can take several hours.

Astronomers gain clues as to the state of the Earth's atmosphere by looking at a lunar eclipse

How the Full Moon's appearance changes as it gracefully enters the shadow of the Earth in space. Longer exposures at totality reveal the colors on the lunar surface in shadow

MERCURY

Mercury – the closest planet to the Sun – is a rocky terrestrial world like Earth. In size and appearance, however, it more closely resembles the Moon. It has a heavily cratered, mountainous surface that has been untouched by weathering, because the planet has only a very tenuous atmosphere.

At a distance averaging around 36 million mi/58 million km from the Sun, Mercury experiences enormous contrasts in temperature. The side facing the Sun gets a severe roasting, reaching 800°F/430°C. The dark side of Mercury becomes a deep freeze, with temperatures plunging to -290°F/-180°C.

Highly reflective areas within the craters lead scientists to believe that there might well be ice within the crater walls, permanently frozen in areas that never receive sunlight.

Mercury spins slowly on its axis, with a day that is around 59 Earth days long. That's not much less than the length of its year, because it zips around the Sun in just 88 days.

This orbit, incidentally, is the most eccentric of the planets, with the Mercury-Sun distance ranging from 28.6 million to 43.5 million mi/ 46 million to 70 million km. Mercury is unique in the

Only one space probe has visited Mercury so far, and it

solar system in that its axis is is at a 90 degree angle to the plane of its orbit, so that there can never be any seasons on the planet. Mercury, named after the winged messenger of the gods, is believed to have had a particularly violent birth. The planet is known to contain unexpectedly high levels of iron. The theory is that this is because it was formed from an impact between a giant asteroid and a much larger world that was orbiting the Sun more than four billion years ago.

Only one space probe has so far visited Mercury –

more than 30 years ago – although things are about to change. America's unmanned Mariner 10 probe made three flybys of the planet in 1974 and 1975, and those brief approaches transformed our knowledge of Mercury.

The probe was able to photograph less than half of Mercury's surface, but the pictures revealed its lunar-like craters plus a system of ridges hundreds of km long which are thought to have formed when the planet originally cooled and shrank. Most prominent among the features is the Caloris basin, a ring of mountains 807 mi/1,300 km high.

Two more robotic missions will unlock more of the secrets of Mercury. A NASA mission called Messenger has been en route there since 2004, but will not go into orbit around the planet until 2011.

Another mission to Mercury, BepiColombo, will carry two orbiters, one European and one Japanese. The craft is not due for launch until 2013 and the probes will not arrive until six years later.

photographed less than half of the planet's total surface

NASA Jet Propulsion Laboratory

OBSERVING MERCURY

Mercury is one of the brightest objects in the heavens, yet many people go through life without ever seeing it. This is because it clings to the so Sun that it is never visible in a truly dark sky. It never manages to get more than 28 degrees from the Sun at one of its elongations and so, from most of the world, it never stands very high above the horizon in the twilight sky. Even when these favorable apparitions occur, the planet is often hidden in low cloud, haze or murk.

The times to look for Mercury are when it reaches its eastern elongation after sunset or western elongation before sunrise.

However, celestial geometry means that the angle of the ecliptic – the imaginary line through the sky along which the Sun and planets appear to travel – is steeper to the horizon at certain times of year than others. The steeper the angle, the better your viewing chances.

For observers in the northern hemisphere, the best evening (eastern) elongations occur in the spring and the best morning (western) elongations are in the autumn. The reverse is the case in the southern hemisphere. If you are viewing in the evening, start looking for Mercury while the sky is still bright. Binoculars will help, but no attempt should be made to use them to sweep for the planet until after the Sun has set.

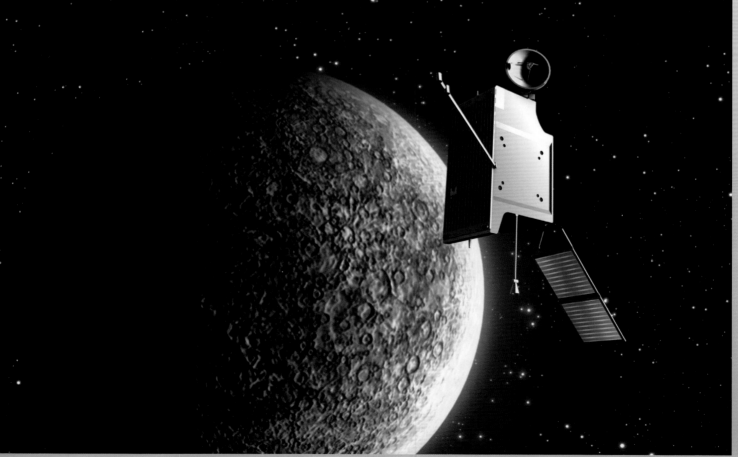

ESA - C.Carreau

"One rare occasion when it is possible to view Mercury is during a transit across the disk of the Sun"

When you do spot Mercury, it resembles a bright star. A telescope with a high-power eyepiece will allow you to distinguish the moon-like phases, but don't expect to see any detail such as mountains and craters – the planet is too far away. Experienced observers sketch Mercury, however, recording subtle shadings on its tiny surface.

There is another rare occasion when it is possible to view Mercury – during a transit, when the planet passes directly in front of the Sun and appears as a silhouette. These are rarer than one might imagine because Mercury's orbit is tilted slightly with respect to ours and so usually passes above or below the Sun. Transits only occur in May or November, with May events happening at intervals of 13 and 33 years and November events at intervals of seven, 13 and 33 years. The next transit will not occur until May 9, 2016, and the next one after that will be on November 11, 2019.

JAXA

Mercury's path across the solar disk on November 8, 2006, as seen from Earth. The transit was best seen from the Pacific. Timings are by the astronomer's favored system, Universal Time.

Observing transits requires the same critical care as observing eclipses of the Sun. Use similar techniques to those described earlier in this book . Mercury will appear as a tiny dark dot crossing the solar disk.

FAR LEFT: *Europe and Japan are planning a joint mission to explore Mercury. Two probes will be launched in 2013 and will take six years before they go into orbit around the heavily cratered planet.*

LEFT: *A spectacular image taken with the Hinode satellite's X-ray telescope shows Mercury closing in for the transit of 2006.*

NASA/ESA

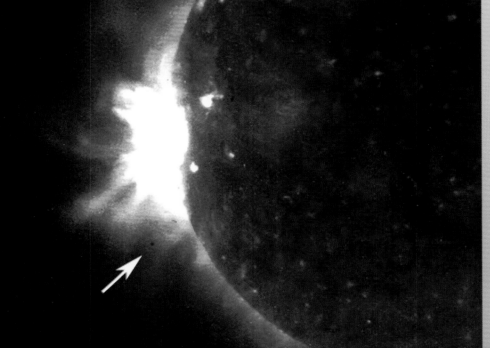

VENUS

There can be few more beautiful sights in nature than that of Venus shining brilliantly in a twilight sky. The second planet from the Sun has a serene splendor explaining why it is named after the Roman goddess of love.

Appearances can be deceptive, however. Venus is, in reality, a planet in poisonous climatic turmoil.

Scientists are fascinated to know why that should be, because it was once believed that Venus could be like Earth. The two worlds are approximately the same size, are both made of rock, have atmospheres and inhabit a similar zone of the solar system. But our closest planetary neighbor is a world whose climate has gone out of control.

The air is heavy with sulfuric acid, the surface glows at 400°C/750°F, twice the maximum temperature inside a domestic oven. Anything surviving that heat would be crushed by the pressure of the atmosphere.

It was only comparatively recently that we learned this, because Venus is enveloped by a dense cover of clouds. The surface of the planet is completely hidden from us and, before the advent of space probes, astronomers could only speculate as to what lay at the surface. Some imagined vast oceans as the source of the clouds. Others suggested it was covered by Saharan-type deserts.

The clouds must reflect around 60 percent of the Sun's light and heat, so its fiery conditions are thought to be due to a runaway greenhouse effect.

Early clues that all was not well on Venus came when the former Soviet Union sent a sequence of probes named Venera to the planet. It was not long before they sent back data revealing Venus's searing temperatures, extreme atmospheric pressure at the surface (90 times greater than on Earth) and raging thunderstorms. Two probes even transmitted images of the planet's rocky terrain in the minutes before they were crushed to destruction.

Later probes managed to lift the veil from Venus even more. Two American Mariner missions learned more about the make-up of the atmosphere — mainly carbon dioxide with some nitrogen — and photographed the patterns in the cloud tops. But the greatest flood of information came when the US spacecraft Magellan sailed into orbit around Venus in 1990 and began to chart its surface in detail, using cloud-penetrating radar.

Europe's Venus Express probe is orbiting the planet and sending back valuable data about its atmosphere, including observations of a powerful double vortex above Venus's south pole.

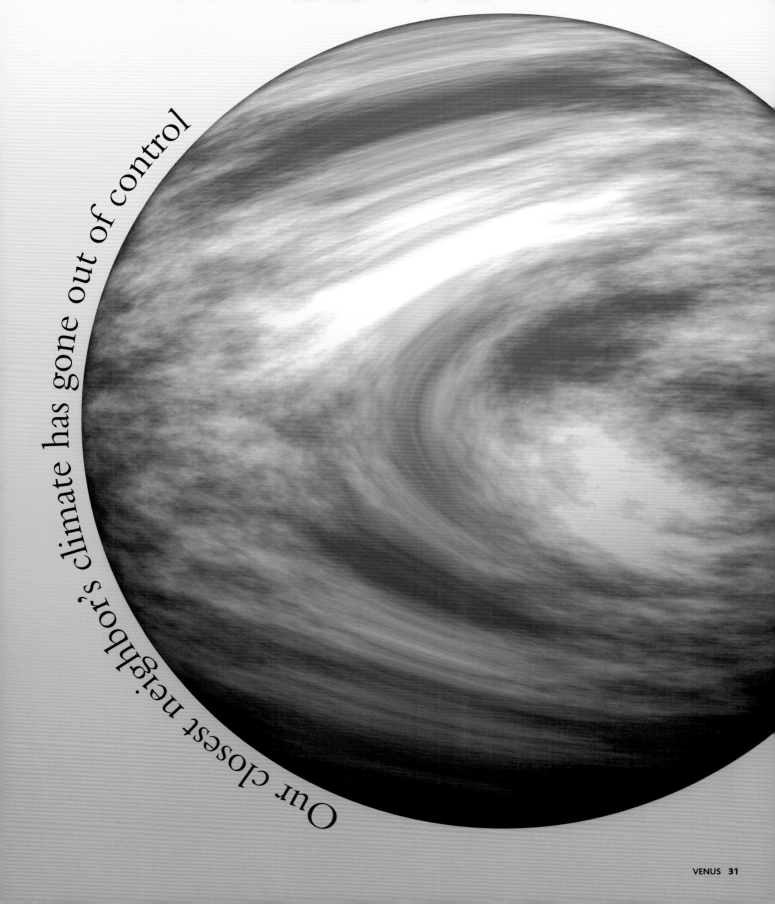

Our closest neighbor's climate has gone out of control

Venus's landscape has volcanoes spewing sulfur dioxide into the atmosphere.

Credit

Magellan was a stunning success, allowing planetary scientists to draw up high-resolution maps of Venus, before the probe was deliberately plunged into the atmosphere in 1994. The maps showed that the totally dry surface was made up mainly of smooth plains with two continent-sized highland areas: one in the northern hemisphere, now named Ishtar Terra, and one in the southern, called Aphrodite Terra.

Most of the mountains and other surface features were named after historical and mythological women, in keeping with the planet's own female persona. The features detected include 167 giant volcanoes and nearly 1,000 impact craters.

In 2006 a European space probe, Venus Express, went into orbit around the planet and began returning fascinating new data, including close-up images of a swirling double vortex over the south pole.

For the amateur astronomer, Venus is an easy if inscrutable target. It can become as bright as magnitude -4.7 – enough to cast a shadow – and is then even visible in daylight in crystal clear skies.

Its moon-like pattern of phases can be seen through a telescope, as Galileo first showed in the 17th century. When Venus lies beyond the Sun, it shows a gibbous (i.e: waxing or waning) face but, when it's at its brightest, it displays a crescent shape that may be seen in binoculars.

Some amateurs have sketched subtle shadings in the atmosphere, but there are not the striking details seen on other planets.

Brilliant Venus, the third brightest object in the sky, makes a beautiful pairing with the crescent Moon in one of its appearances as the so-called Evening Star.

One phenomenon seen by various experienced observers is the so-called Ashen Light, a mysterious glowing of the dark part of the planet that is in shadow and should therefore be invisible. Discounting the possibility of an illusion, it has been suggested this could be due to lightning in the continually raging thunderstorms. Others wonder if it is caused by volcanic eruptions or is perhaps a glow from the baking landscape.

Venus lies an average of 68 million mi/ 109 million km from the Sun and, from Earth, appears to venture as far as 47 degrees from it in the sky when at either its eastern elongation, in the evening, or western elongation, in the morning. This means that, unlike Mercury, it may at times be seen shining in a dark sky.

Because Venus's orbit is inclined slightly to our own, it usually passes above or below the solar disk when at inferior or superior conjunction. However, at rare intervals, it may be seen gliding across the Sun's disk as a large black dot. This last happened on June 8, 2004, and will happen again on June 6, 2012.

"One of Venus's mysteries is the so-called Ashen Light, a mysterious glowing of the dark part of the planet that is in shadow and should therefore be invisible"

Venus takes 224.7 days to complete one orbit of the Sun. But a final oddity is that its own day (the time it takes to spin on its axis) is 243 days – longer than its year. It also rotates in the opposite direction to other planets in the solar system. Venus is a strange world indeed.

Mars has come under intense scrutiny from space probes

MARS

Mars, often known as the Red Planet, fascinates people because it most resembles Earth. Although a lot smaller – just 4,222mi/6,795km wide – it is made of rock, has an atmosphere, albeit thinner than ours, and experiences weather. Why is it red? Because the surface is covered with rust – or iron oxide.

Mars has a day just 40 minutes longer than Earth's, and on its nearly two-year long journey around the Sun it enjoys seasons similar to ours because its axis is tilted 25 degrees, in a similar way to our own.

There are also, we are beginning to discover, significant reserves of water on Mars. Scientists are intrigued to know, therefore, whether the planet might ever have been home to life – and whether life might still exist there today.

It's no surprise, then, that Mars has been put under greater scrutiny by space probes than any other planet. Several are already in orbit around it and others have landed and

sent robots trundling across its surface. The planet is also a target for a manned mission within the next few decades.

Thanks to the probes' cameras and other instruments, we are being deluged with detailed information about our planetary

neighbor. Martian features include the biggest volcano in the solar system, the 16mi/26km high Olympus Mons, plus Valles Marineris, a vast chasm 2,500mi/4,000km long that dwarfs the Earth's Grand Canyon.

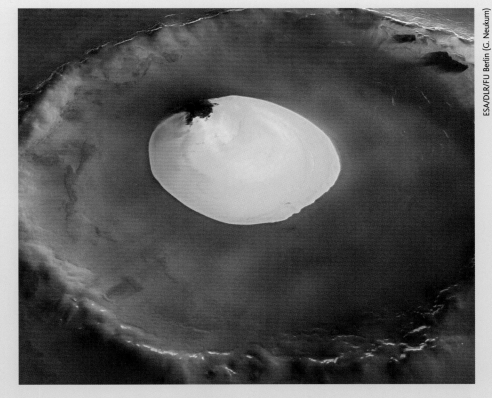

ESA/DLR/FU Berlin (G. Neukum)

Left: Europe's Rosetta spaceprobe swung past Mars on its way to chase a comet and radioed back to Earth this image of the Red Planet.

A large patch of water ice is photographed by Europe's Mars Express probe on the floor of a crater in the Vastitas Borealis region in the high northern latitudes of Mars.

The planet is also dotted with craters from asteroid impacts, first spotted when NASA's Mariner 4 flew past Mars in 1965. Recent monitoring of the surface shows that smaller impacts are still occurring today.

Unlike the Moon, Mars' surface is constantly weathered by winds. Deserts reveal the familiar patterns of sand dunes, and little whirlwinds called dust devils whip across the surface. Every couple of years or so, and thanks to seasonal temperature changes, much bigger dust storms blow up, sometimes enveloping the entire planet.

The notion that aliens might exist on Mars received a major boost in the late 19th century when Italian astronomer Giovanni Schiaparelli announced that he had seen channels on Mars. His Italian was wrongly translated into English as "canals". American astronomer Sir Percival Lowell "confirmed" their existence and claimed there was vegetation growing alongside waterways.

We now know these Martian waterways were simply an optical illusion. But the truth, we are learning, is no less exciting. There is plenty of evidence for water on Mars, and planetary scientists believe it was once a blue planet under vast oceans, just like Earth.

Many Martian features, including channels and gullies, appear to have been sculpted by running water. Other features show sediment deposits. An area near the equator resembles a frozen sea, with the shapes of ice floes clearly visible through the sand. And most remarkably, the American space agency NASA revealed picture evidence in 2006 of fresh deposits that indicated water was still bursting from below the surface and running down crater slopes before evaporating into space.

Certainly, there is still much water at the poles. Studies by a ground-piercing radar instrument on Europe's Mars Express orbiter showed that the southern polar cap holds enough ice to cover the planet with a sea 36ft/11m deep.

Two robot rovers, Spirit and Opportunity, which landed on Mars in January 2004, both found conclusive evidence of features formed by the presence of water. Future international missions are being planned to land on Mars and bring rock samples back for detailed analysis. Strict quarantine measures will have to be observed to protect the samples from terrestrial contamination.

ESA

The ExoMars rover is just one of the ways space agencies are planning to explore the surface of Mars further.

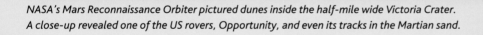

NASA

NASA's Mars Reconnaissance Orbiter pictured dunes inside the half-mile wide Victoria Crater. A close-up revealed one of the US rovers, Opportunity, and even its tracks in the Martian sand.

DEIMOS AND PHOBOS

Mars has two moons, named Phobos (top) and Deimos (bottom). Their small sizes and irregular shapes mean they appear more like asteroids captured by the planet's gravitational pull, and indeed most astronomers believe that is what they are. Phobos, which is just 16.8mi/27km long, has distinctive groove markings thought to have been gouged out by material ejected from Mars in an impact. Deimos is even smaller, at 9.3mi/15km long. Both moons are covered with craters.

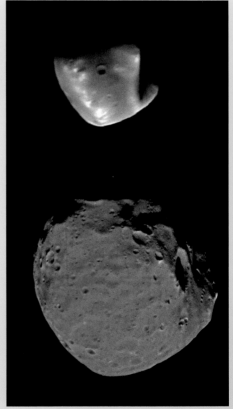

NASA

However, it appears there are samples of Mars already on Earth. We know of a number of meteorites with a chemistry that shows they must have been blasted out of the Martian surface, perhaps by an asteroid impact, and then floated around space for aeons before falling to Earth.

One such meteorite lay preserved in Antarctica, and caused a sensation in 1996 when NASA scientists claimed it contained microscopic, worm-like bacteria.

Closer inspection has led most scientists to conclude that these aliens are the result of contamination on Earth.

Even if that is the case, more and more scientists now believe we will find evidence of microbial life forms on Mars, especially as organisms have been found to survive in the most extreme conditions, including volcanic vents, radioactive sites and even the vacuum of space. Future exploration of Mars will be fascinating.

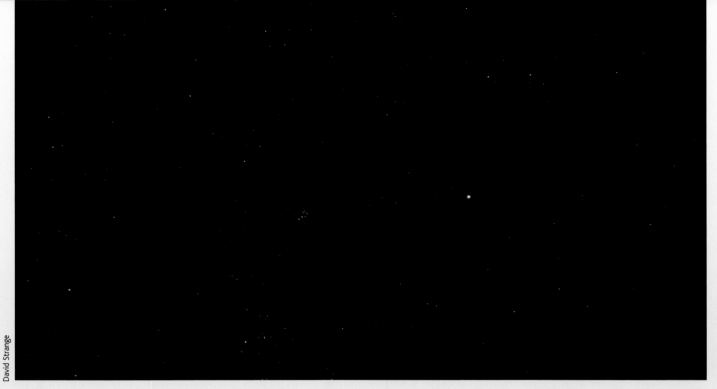

Mars hangs brilliantly in the night sky close to the Pleiades and Hyades star clusters in Taurus around the time of one of its favorable Oppositions. At other times Mars is seen much fainter.

OBSERVING MARS

Mars can be explored with even a small telescope, particularly for a period of a few weeks every couple of years or so, when Earth and Mars come closest together. In the intervening year, Mars lies on the far side of the Sun during its 687-day long journey around it. The circumstances of our neighboring orbits means that the distance between the Earth and Mars varies hugely.

But when Mars is at Opposition and therefore at its closest, it becomes one of the brightest objects in the sky, sometimes reaching a magnitude of -2.8. It is then easy to see why it was dubbed the Red Planet and given the name of the Roman god of war, because it hangs like a drop of blood in the heavens.

Around opposition, Mars becomes a sizeable object that is rewarding to observe even through a modest amateur telescope. Its apparent diameter can reach as much as 25 arcseconds across, compared to a tiny 3.5 arcseconds when it is on the other side of the Sun. Some oppositions are better than others, because Mars' elliptical orbit means its closest distance from Earth can vary between 34 million and 62 million mi/ 55 million and 100 million km. At the most unfavorable oppositions, it can reach a diameter of only 14 arcseconds.

During these close encounters, amateur astronomers can spot the white patches marking the polar ice caps and the dark shadings of major features such as Syrtis Major, a V-shaped region resembling the Indian sub-continent.

These dark markings were first noticed by Italian astronomers in the early 17th century, following the invention of the telescope. Galileo viewed Mars through his in 1610, noting its sometimes gibbous shape. In 1636, his countryman Francesco Fontana made the first recorded sketch of the planet's features.

Traditional observers still make sketches of Mars, filling in printed templates provided by national astronomical societies. There is undoubtedly a great sense of achievement to be had from making one's own visual log in this way. But the development of webcam-style devices and more sophisticated CCD cameras, as well as software with which to process images, are leading more and more amateurs to keep a photographic record of the Red Planet.

Olympus Mons, pictured here by NASA's Viking 1 orbiter, is the largest volcano known in the solar system. It has a diameter of around 360mi/600km and the caldera at the summit stands 15mi/24km above the surrounding plains at three times the height of Everest.

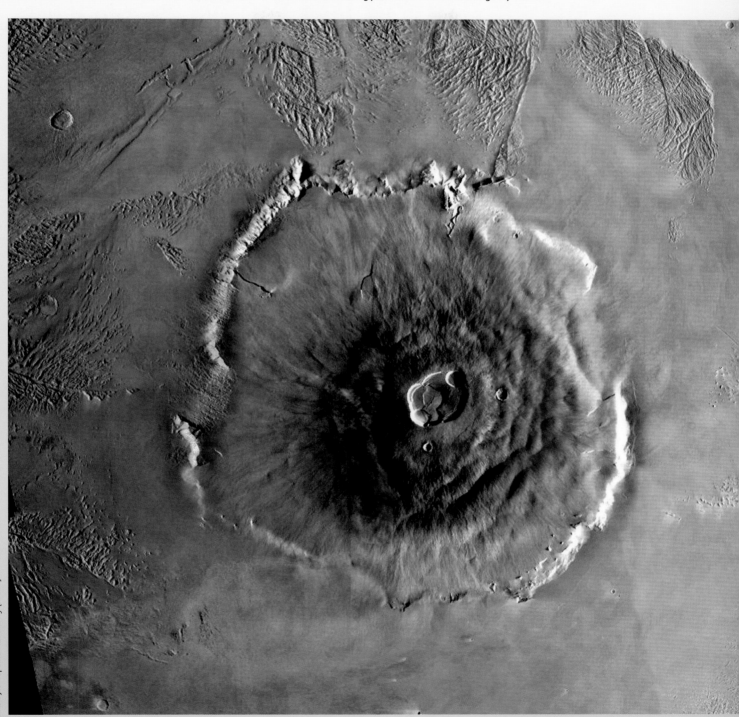

NASA Jet Propulsion Laboratory (NASA-JP

ASTEROIDS

Hundreds of asteroids of varying size travel on orbits which pass just a few tens of millions of miles from that of the Earth.

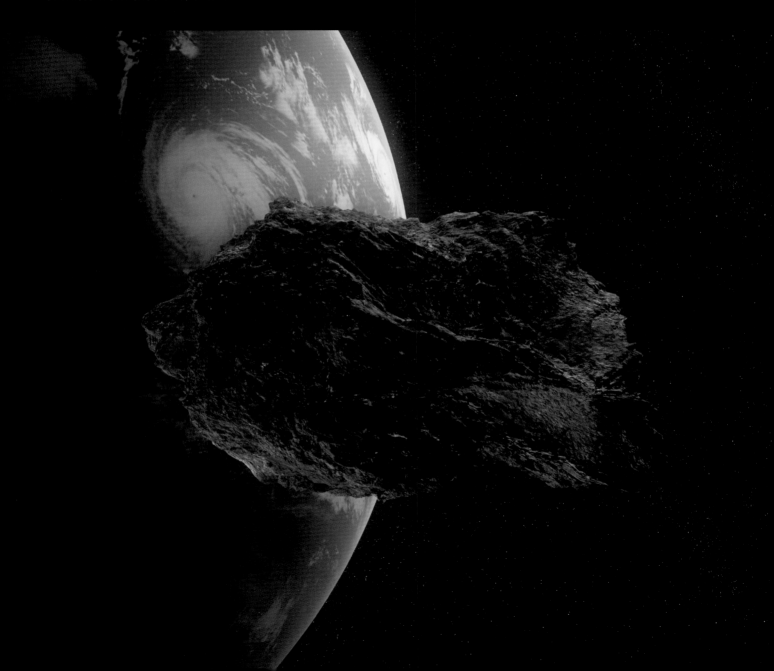

Automatic telescopes constantly monitor the sky to detect and track threatening objects, and space missions are being planned to fly out and deal with them. Many hundreds of asteroids of varying sizes travel on orbits that cross or pass close to that of the Earth. But the vast majority – probably 95 percent – steer well clear of us as they orbit the Sun in a zone called the Asteroid Belt.

This cosmic highway lies between the orbits of Mars and Jupiter and is littered with hundreds of thousands of rocks half a mile or more in size, and usually irregularly shaped. They fill a gap in the solar system where one might expect another planet to lie. The first were discovered after a group of 24 astronomers with the wonderful name of the Celestial Police searched for such a missing planet in the late 18th century. The first spotted – by Giuseppe Piazzi, in Sicily in 1801 – was Ceres. It is the largest asteroid, with a diameter of about 590mi/950km, and it orbits the Sun once every 4.6 years.

Subsequently other large asteroids were discovered, including the 380mi/610km wide Pallas and the 340mi/540km wide Vesta. The latter is the only asteroid that usually which bright enough to be seen by the naked eye. Hundreds of thousands of asteroids have since been discovered, usually in photographs; the current rate of detection is around 5,000 a month. Still, it's estimated that even if they were all combined in one, they would form a body less than half the size of the Moon.

It was thought that asteroids were produced when a planet was pulled to pieces by

Gaspra was the first asteroid to be seen close-up, pictured by the Galileo probe to Jupiter

collisions or gravitational forces but modern thinking is that the rocks are remains of the early disk of material that collected to form the solar system. The rocks in the asteroids' space lanes never managed to combine because of the disruptive gravitational effects of mighty neighbor Jupiter. Jupiter has also managed to shepherd clusters of asteroid into special regions ahead and behind itself in its own orbit. These clusters, at regions known as the Lagrangian points in the orbit, are known as Trojans.

Asteroids are often referred to as Minor Planets, but in 2006, our contemporary celestial police force, the International Astronomical Union, decreed that they be officially known as small Solar System bodies. At the same time, Ceres was promoted to a new category: Dwarf Planet.

Though the largest and earliest-found asteroids, like the planets, have classical names, they are also identified by catalogue numbers. It has become traditional also for the myriad of smaller rocks to be awarded names of living people, in recognition of their achievements.

Space probes have given us our first close-up views of asteroids with a number of flybys. The first came in 1991, when Galileo, on the way to Jupiter, sped past a space rock called Gaspra. It showed it to be a tumbling, elongated body, solid and about 11mi/17km long, its surface dotted with impact craters. Other probes have checked out Ida, which was found to have its own tiny moon called Dactyl, and Eros, among others. In 2005, Japan's Hayabusa probe touched down briefly on Itokawa, collecting samples from its surface.

Many asteroids, including Ceres, Pallas and Vesta, can be spotted easily with binoculars. You can check where to find them in astronomical magazines or via national societies. The number on view increases vastly when you use a telescope. None will appear as any more than a point of light, but it can be fascinating to watch how they move against the starry background from onenight to the next.

Asteroids drift through the space lanes between Mars and Jupiter, far from the Sun.

JUPITER

Jupiter is the undisputed king of the planets and the first of the so-called gas giants. It has a diameter at the equator of almost 88,860mi/43,000km although, rather oddly, the distance measured between the poles is a lot less at 83,260mi/134,000km, making the planet resemble a pumpkin. This is due to Jupiter's rapid rotation – the planet spins so fast that a day is under 10 Earth hours long.

Jupiter lies an average 485 million mi/ 780 million km from the Sun and its light takes more than 40 minutes to reach us. Such is its size that it is one of the brightest objects in the heavens, earning it the name of the chief Roman god.

The gas clouds at Jupiter's surface are impenetrable by any telescopes, but it's thought that, deep inside the planet, there could be a solid rocky core up to 12,500mi/20,000km across. Those veils of cloud – mainly hydrogen and helium with traces of methane, ammonia and ethane – offer a fascinating canvas of color.

A look through even a modest amateur telescope will reveal that Jupiter shows a pattern of horizontal stripes. Close-up photos show these to be a multi-hued extravaganza of weather systems, with bands of high-speed winds blowing in opposite directions. Following the changing shapes and intensities of the swirling features makes Jupiter fascinating to study.

None of those features is more dramatic than Jupiter's famous Great Red Spot, a raging storm so vast that it has been observed for centuries and shows no sign of diminishing. This spot, which varies in redness over time, is up to 24,850mi/ 40,000km long and 8,700mi/14,000km wide. It is big enough to swallow the Earth three times over.

In the early 21st century, another, smaller red spot was seen to form, but most storms on Jupiter tend to be white or brown in colour and last days, months or years.

Johns Hopkins University Applied Physics Lab

Although the main mission of NASA's New Horizons is to explore the Pluto system and the Kuiper Belt of icy, rocky objects, the spacecraft first flew by the solar system's largest planet.

Jupiter's colored bands are the result of high-speed winds

Io, one of the four major Galilean satellites of Jupiter, casts its shadow on the planet's colorful cloudtops close to the famous Great Red Spot.

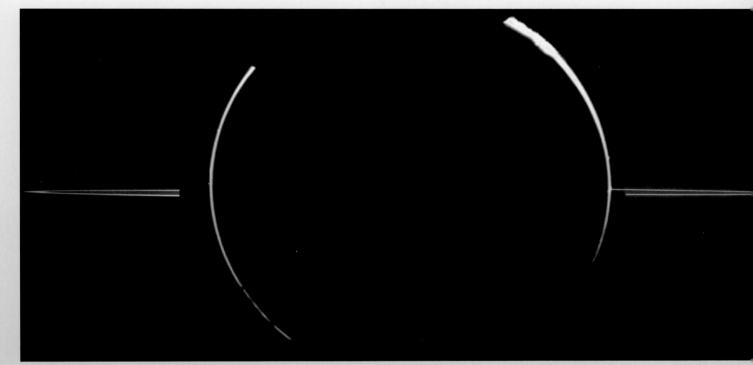

A dramatic view of the rings of Jupiter taken by the Galileo probe as it flew around the back of the planet, viewed from the side in shadow from the Sun. Its limb is lit up by scattered sunlight.

Jupiter shines by reflecting sunlight. However, it emits more than twice as much energy as it receives from the Sun and radio telescopes find it one of the noisiest objects in the sky. Astronomers believe Jupiter's energy is produced from the forces of it shrinking from a much larger world many millions of years ago. The planet also has a powerful magnetic field.

Space probes, either in orbit or passing by, have helped us learn a lot more about Jupiter. They have discovered that it has faint rings, which are made up of tiny dust particles fed into them from meteor impacts on satellites in its own extended family.

This family consists of 63 natural satellites, although many discovered in recent years are tiny fragments of rock captured by the planet's powerful gravitational pull.

There are, however, four sizeable moons. They are so big that they would have ranked as planets if they had orbited the Sun alone. These Big Four – Io, Europa, Ganymede and Callisto – are called the Galilean satellites because it was Galileo who discovered them in 1610. They are clearly visible through binoculars, stretched in a line around Jupiter like a string of pearls. It can be fascinating to watch their changing pattern as they orbit their home world.

Ganymede is the biggest moon in the solar system, with a diameter of 3,270mi/ 5,262km. Its surface is covered with craters, grooves and ridges.

Callisto is 2,996mi/4,821km wide. Jupiter's second largest moon has a heavily cratered surface covering a thick layer of ice.

Spacecraft views of Io show it resembling a pizza, due to the eruptions that make it the most volcanically active world in the solar system. It has a diameter of 2,264mi/3,643km.

Europa – 1,940mi/3,122km across – fascinates planetary scientists because it is a smooth satellite spewing geysers of water ice. Some believe a vast underground lake could contain simple aquatic life.

SATURN

The sixth planet from the Sun, Saturn is a fast-spinner like Jupiter, with a day less than 11 hours long. It is the second largest planet, with an equatorial diameter of 74,898mi/120,536km and resembles its larger neighbor, being squashed at the poles and completely circled by bands of cloud.

The rings around Saturn are thought to have formed from material that was unable to form into a moon because of tidal forces from Saturn, or from a Moon that was broken up.

"Even a small telescope will show Saturn's incredible rings"

Saturn's most striking feature, however, is a spectacular ring system marking it out as the most beautiful object in the heavens. The smallest telescope displays the rings. Galileo was first to spot them in 1610, although he thought he was observing three separate round objects. He must have had a better telescope in 1616, because his sketch made then clearly shows the ring system.

Larger instruments confirmed that there is more than one ring, including the 2,485mi/4,000km wide Cassini Division. But photos from space probes have shown that there are countless rings made up of tiny particles of pulverized rock ranging in size from specks to boulders. These are held in check by the pull of Saturn's many satellites.

Saturn itself is a gas giant like Jupiter. The cloud bands are less colorful than Jupiter's, and the features more subtle, but they include oval storms which break out occasionally and a Great White Spot which was first noticed in 1876 and appears to recur at roughly 30-year intervals.

NASA Marshall Space Flight Center

Our knowledge of Saturn, its rings and its moons has been given a huge boost by the arrival of the space probe Cassini in 2004. This American-European mission has been viewing the Saturn family from every angle since then. Among its discoveries are odd storm systems at the planet's north and south poles. The southern hurricane is two-thirds the size of the Earth, with a well-developed eye. The one at the north pole is shaped like a hexagon with six straight sides. Nothing like it has been observed on any of the other planets.

Saturn has a vast retinue of natural satellites – at least 56 discovered so far. Of these, there are six major moons: Mimas, Enceladus, Tethys, Dione, Rhea and Titan.

With a massive crater Mimas resembles the Death Star from Star Wars. The crater, blasted out by an asteroid impact, is named Herschel after William Herschel, who first spotted Mimas in 1789. The moon is only 246mi/396km across. Herschel also spotted Enceladus, a 311mi/500km wide world which fascinates scientists investigating the possibility of life elsewhere in the solar system. The Cassini space probe showed plumes of water ice erupting from its smooth, reflective surface, indicating that it is geologically active. There could be an underground sea where primitive life might exist or be evolving.

Tethys, discovered by the astronomer Cassini in 1684, is another icy world, 665mi/1,070km in diameter and covered with craters and cracks, the largest of which is the 250mi/400km diameter Odysseus.

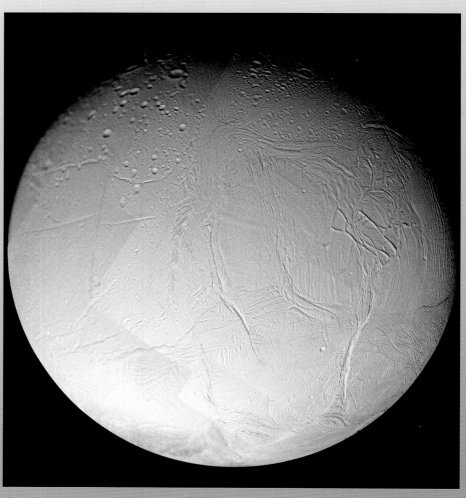

This 16-image mosaic of Enceladus was taken during Cassini's first close flyby of this moon of Saturn on February 17 2005.

Another striking feature is the 60mi/100km wide valley Ithaca Chasma, which is 1,240mi/2,000km long and runs about three quarters of the way around the moon.

Dione – width 700mi/1,120km and also discovered by Cassini – is another world with vast amounts of water ice. As well as extensive cratering, there are also long streaks which indicate cliffs of ice.

Rhea is the third of Cassini's moons and Saturn's second largest with a diameter of 950mi/1,530km. Like Dione, it is covered with craters and ice cliffs. Saturn's biggest moon, Titan, is also the second largest in the solar system. With a diameter of 3,200mi/5,150km, it is half as big again as our own Moon and larger than the planet Mercury.

An artist's interpretation of the area surrounding the Huygens landing site on Titan based on images and data returned on January 14 2005.

Titan has recently come under greater scrutiny than any other moon because it appears in many ways to resemble a young Earth. The research has culminated with the landing of a European space probe, Huygens, in January 2005, after it had flown piggyback to Saturn on NASA's Cassini orbiter.

Titan is the only planetary satellite with a dense atmosphere, which shows as an orange haze in photographs. After floating to the slushy surface by parachute, during which it recorded the winds and photographed coastlines, rivers and deltas, Huygens took images of a landscape covered in icy rocks and pebbles. One rock appeared broken and may have been fractured when the probe bounced off it.

Radar images from the Cassini mothership showed seas and lakes in Titan's northern hemisphere. These are not lakes as we know them, but filled with liquid methane or ethane. Scientists believe there may be an underground sea on Titan where the organic ingredients for life are present. It could be a balmy place to live in another four billion years, by which time the Sun is expected to swell into a red giant.

URANUS, NEPTUNE & PLUTO

The axis of Uranus is tilted at nearly 98 degrees

Until little more than two centuries ago, we only knew of the planets visible to the naked eye; those that stretch as far as Saturn.

Uranus was spotted in 1781 by William Herschel, a scientist, telescope builder and musician, as he was observing the night skies from his garden in England's historic city of Bath. Others had previously noted it in their observation logs but thought it just another star.

Herschel wanted to name his planet Georgium Sidus, in a tribute to King George III. But protocol dictated that the new world was given a classical name just like the rest.

Uranus is 32,000mi/51,200km wide and 1,800 million mi/2,900 million km from the Sun, and just bright enough to be glimpsed with the naked eye on a clear, dark night. It is, however, so close to the limit of visibility that it's not difficult to see how it remained undetected for so long.

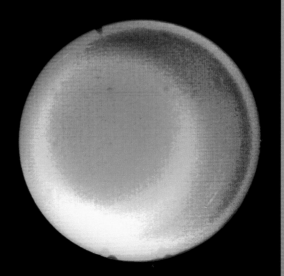

RIGHT *Uranus's atmosphere viewed by Voyager 2.*

NASA Jet Propulsion Laboratory (NASA-JPL)

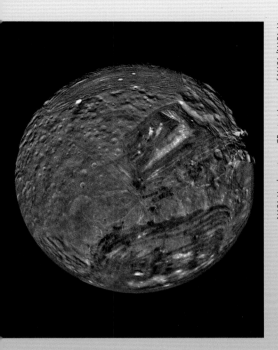

NASA Headquarters - GReatest Images of NASA (NASA-H

NASA's Voyager 2 probe has given us our only close-up view Uranus's moon Miranda.

Neptune was found by maths before it was seen

Binoculars show it easily and a telescope will delineate a tiny blue-green disk. They won't show any details, but a few nights of noting Uranus's position against the stars will reveal the slow movement on its 84-year journey around the Sun.

Uranus is another of the gas giants of the solar system, being made mainly of hydrogen and helium plus a hint of methane, though its cloud tops are pretty bland visually, compared to the multi-colored Jupiter.

It has five main moons: Ariel, Umbriel, Oberon, Titania and the baby of the group, Miranda. Larger amateur telescopes will show them as faint dots. There are at least another 22, much tinier satellites in orbit.

Another development occured in 1977 when astronomers were watching Uranus pass in front of a star in what is termed an occultation. The star blinked on and off repeatedly, revealing the presence of rings around it. The space probe Voyager 2 confirmed their existence in 1986. As with Jupiter's rings, they are totally inconspicuous, unlike the splendid rings around Saturn.

Uranus has another curious feature. Its polar axis, around which it spins in a day lasting 17 and a quarter hours, is tilted right over at nearly 98 degrees. It is likely that it collided with another giant body long ago.

A matter of 60 or so years after Herschel's discovery the solar system grew once again with the confirmation of the eighth planet, Neptune, in 1846. This find was remarkable because it came as a result of mathematical calculation rather than a sweep of the heavens.

Triton is the largest of Neptune's moons and was photographed by NASA's Voyager 2 spaceprobe when it flew past in 1989, revealing that the moon is a rocky world covered by an icy mantle. This montage shows Triton in the foreground with gas giant Neptune itself in the distance.

Observations of Uranus had shown that it was not maintaining its expected orbit. The pull of another, as yet unknown body, was blamed. Astronomers in the UK and France independently predicted where the culprit lay, and Frenchman Urbain Le Verrier just beat Englishman John Couch Adams to the declaration. Final confirmation came when astronomers at Berlin Observatory spotted Neptune close to the spot where it was predicted to lie.

Yet another world of gas, Neptune could easily pass as a twin of Uranus. It is slightly smaller at 31,000mi/49,500km wide and so far away at a distance of 2.8 billion miles/ 4.5 billion km that it takes 165 years to orbit the Sun.

Neptune reaches magnitude 7.8 at its best, but it may be picked out with binoculars. Like Uranus, Neptune has a faint ring system, which was first detected during an

occultation of a star in 1983. Its day is a fraction over 16 hours long.

Neptune has two main moons — Triton and Nereid — and at least 11 much smaller ones. Triton is the biggest, with a diameter of 1,680mi/2,700km, and orbits the "wrong way" around Neptune. It is also slowly spiraling in toward the planet, and will eventually shatter to form another ring of debris.

Nereid is only 211mi/340km across and has an extremely stretched orbit that takes it nearly seven times further from Neptune at certain times.

Neptune is the last of the Sun's main family of planets. Until August 2006, there was a ninth planet, Pluto, which was demoted by the astronomical authorities to the new status of Dwarf Planet.

This controversial decision sparked a wave of protest, particularly in the United States, where Pluto was discovered by Clyde Tombaugh in 1930. Legislators in New Mexico passed a motion declaring Pluto to be a planet again in 2007, although they had no authority to do so.

The decision to reduce Pluto's status was, in fact, logical. Astronomers had begun to discover a number of similar new icy bodies in the same outer fringes of the solar system, suggesting Pluto had received special treatment for historical reasons. More than 800 have been found so far, and some may turn out to be larger than Pluto.

This region of space it termed the Kuiper Belt, and it is thought the giant planets hold a vast number of small icy bodies in position there. They are unlike the asteroids but are probably one source of the comets which frequently fly in toward the Sun.

With a diameter of 1,500mi/2,400km, Pluto is smaller than many of the solar system's moons, including our own. Its eccentric orbit means its distance from the Sun varies between 2.7 billion and 4.5 billion miles/4.3 billion and 7.3 billion km, and it takes 248 years to complete one revolution.

Pluto has three natural satellites. Charon is just over half Pluto's diameter. Two much smaller moons, Nix and Hydra, were spotted by the Hubble space telescope in 2005.

A NASA mission, called New Horizons, is currently on its way to explore Pluto and the Kuiper Belt but will not arrive until 2015.

"Until August 2006, there was a ninth planet, Pluto which was demoted by astronomical authorities to the new status of Dwarf Planet"

An artist's impression of Pluto, which will be visited for the first time by a spaceprobe in 2015.

COMETS

On August 7, 2006, Rob McNaught, a Scottish astronomer living in Australia, spotted a faint smudge on a photo of the sky taken with a large telescope. Later photos showed the smudge had moved slightly – it was a comet heading towards the Sun from the depths of space.

Sebastian Deiries (ESO)

Comet McNaught: spectacular in January 2007.

The comet became lost from view as it moved into the daylight from Earth, but when it was next seen against a dark sky, in late December, it became clear that it was going to be a bright object in the New Year's skies.

For observers in the northern hemisphere, Comet McNaught became a lovely sight low in the evening twilight. Then, as it rounded the Sun, its head became so brilliant that it could be seen in broad daylight. In the next few days, the comet put on a spectacular show for lucky viewers in the southern hemisphere.

As Comet McNaught moved away from the Sun again, it was a stunning sight in the dusk, sporting a long, sweeping tail that stretched far across the sky. So far, in fact, that though the comet's head was out of sight from northern latitudes, parts of the tail could be viewed in dark skies north of the equator.

Over the next few weeks, Comet McNaught gradually faded and the tail became less glorious as it began to head into the depths of space to become once more a faint, distant smudge.

McNaught had not been seen before, and it may never again return to the heart of the solar system. The last Great Comet, Hale-Bopp in 1997, came as a similar surprise. But a study of its orbit revealed that it had passed through our skies before – 4,200 years ago. During the last flyby, Hale-Bopp's orbit was disrupted by the gravitational pull of giant planet Jupiter,

so that its next return will be somewhat sooner, but still not until around 4380.

Many comets are known to appear at intervals of a few to several years because they, too, have fallen under the spell of Jupiter. In 1993, one of these periodic comets, called Shoemaker-Levy, was seen to break into a number of fragments which the following year crashed one by one into Jupiter's atmosphere, leaving it with long-lasting "black eyes".

The periodic comet with the shortest orbital period is Encke, which takes just 3.3 years to travel around the Sun.

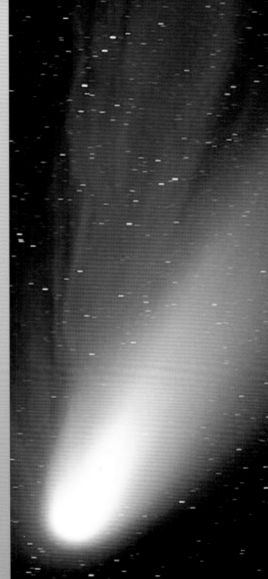

"In 1993, Shoemaker–Levy broke into fragments which, the following year, crashed into Jupiter."

A close-up of Comet Hale-Bopp shows its tails of gas and dust.

NASA Jet Propulsion Laboratory (NASA-JPL)

RIDING A TRAIL OF DEBRIS

This infrared picture taken by NASA's heat-seeking Spitzer Space Telescope shows Comet Encke riding along the diagonal dusty trail of debris that it leaves as it orbits the Sun between Mars and Jupiter. Two bright jets of freshly ejected material can be seen streaming from the comet's head.

Comet Hale-Bopp was a fine subject for photographers. Here is it seen above a tree on the Istrian coast of Croatia. The Andromeda Galaxy can be seen faintly beneath it.

By tradition, comets take the names of their discoverers. Automated cameras are beginning to pick up more and more of these celestial wanderers, meaning that there is an ever-growing list of comets called Linear or Neat. Each is given a catalogue description too, such as C/2006 P1 in the case of Comet McNaught.

Perhaps the most famous visitor is Halley's Comet, which has been witnessed since early historical times and returns to the Sun's neighborhood every 76 years. The closest it came in recent times was 1986 and will be back in 2061. In this case the comet is named not for its discoverer but for Edmond Halley, the man who first recognized that

comets seen in the past were one and the same, and so predicted its reappearance in 1757.

McNaught and Hale-Bopp were truly Great Comets of the kind that come along a handful of times in a lifetime. Less magnificent comets appear fairly often, and one or two a year may become bright enough to be seen with binoculars, or even occasionally with the naked eye. The vast majority appear simply as fuzzy blobs; this is the halo around the head that is called the coma. Only the brightest develop evident tails.

Bright comets show two distinct types of tail: the gas tail and the dust tail. The gas tail is blown from the comet's head by the force of the solar wind. This means that, contrary to what you might expect, this tail does not necessarily follow the comet. As it heads back out towards the depths of the solar system, the comet travels tail-first.

The second tail is formed of the dust that is ejected from the comet's head. It tends to curve as the tiny particles are spread back along the comet's track, to disperse eventually along its orbit. You can read more about these dust particles in the next section.

The gas tail typically shows as blue in photographs, while the dust tail shows as red. This difference was clearly seen in the pictures of Hale-Bopp in 1997, although the colors are often very subtle. Amateur astronomers often sketch comets, noting how condensed the coma is and whether

it has a bright central point. If there are tails, careful observation may reveal the delicate structure within as the gas streams are shaped by the solar wind. Bright comets can also be fine targets for photographers.

Some amateurs also search for new comets by sweeping the skies with giant binoculars or telescopes, a task which requires great dedication and endless patience.

> McNaught and Hale-Bopp were truly Great Comets which appear in a handful of times in a lifetime

A CCD photo of a comet discovered with a robot telescope called NEAT in 2001

WHAT IS A COMET?

Unlike the planets, comets travel in extremely elongated orbits that can bring them from the far realms of the solar system, only to be flung around the Sun and hurled back out into the depths of space. Despite their sometimes spectacular appearance, with tails that can stretch far across the sky, they are relatively insubstantial members of the solar system.

Comets are important because they are believed to contain pristine material older than the Earth, from the earliest days of the solar system. Scientists believe comets may have delivered the water that makes up Earth's oceans — and possibly even the organic material that sparked life itself.

Astronomers believe that comets with orbital periods of just a few hundred years come from the Kuiper Belt of frozen bodies near Pluto. But those that swoop in just once, or once every few thousand years, come from a swarm of billions of comet called the Oort Cloud which is predicted to lie around a light year from the Sun.

The heart of a comet is a frozen mass of rock and ice, usually no bigger than a mountain, that appears as little more than a blob of light when deep in space. But as it approaches the Sun, its frozen core begins to warm and wake up. A huge ball of gas expands to give the comet its hazy coma. Violent jets of gas and dust may erupt from

NASA Jet Propulsion Laboratory (NASA-JPL)

An artist's impression of Deep Impact probe at Comet Tempel 1

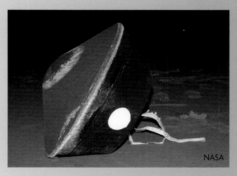

NASA

Another US spacecraft, called Stardust, flew through the coma of Wild 2 and then sent a capsule containing samples of its dust to a soft landing back on Earth in January 2006.

the frozen core, called the nucleus, spewing the material that forms the tails.

Space probes now provide us with a wealth of information about comets. There have been a number of flybys since Giotto sped past Halley's Comet on its last return. Most spectacular was Deep Impact, when NASA deliberately fired a missile at a comet called Tempel 1 in July 2005. The resulting explosion, with the force of 4.5 tons of TNT, caused a brilliant flare visible 83 million miles away on Earth.

NASA's Stardust mission was the first to visit a comet and then return samples to Earth. The probe collected gas and dust surrounding the head of Comet Wild 2 in 2004, then flew by Earth, dropping this capsule into the Utah Desert in 2006.

METEORS

Spend more than a few minutes studying a clear dark sky and you will undoubtedly see one of nature's natural fireworks, a meteor.

Often known as shooting or falling stars, meteors are simply pieces of cosmic debris blazing to a fiery death as they vaporize about 60mi/100km above the Earth.

We now know that most of this debris is the dust shed by comets as they cross the interplanetary space lanes. Some is from long-lost comets which we can no longer identify. Other displays may be linked to comets appearing in our skies today.

What might seem a bright streak is usually caused by just a tiny speck, no bigger than a grain of sand. As its zips through our atmosphere at up to 45mi/70km per second, it ionizes the air around it, causing the brilliant glow. Sometimes this glow will produce a long-lasting ghostly train for several seconds.

Technically, the particle itself is a meteoroid and the streak in the sky is a meteor. Meteoroids from comets are almost invariably destroyed by their blaze of glory. Objects termed meteorites are stones that have survived a fall to Earth and are more likely to be linked to the asteroids. A space rock big enough to reach the ground will produce a fireball in the sky.

NASA

A brilliant fireball bursts from the constellation of Leo during the Leonid storm of 1999.

Meteors may appear at random, in any part of the sky and at any time. However, there are particular periods in the year when we can predict a higher level of meteor activity. These are dates when, each year, the Earth crosses the orbit of a stream of dust left by a comet. The result is what called a meteor shower. The word "shower" is something of an exaggeration because you will rarely see more than one or two a minute. The number will depend not only on how much dust is entering the atmosphere but also on how dark the sky is and whether there is bright moonlight, for example.

Meteors not linked to showers are called sporadics. They are distinguished by the fact that they appear to radiate from a particular

Leo Stachowicz

"There are periods during the year when a higher level of meteor activity is easily predicted — when the Earth crosses the orbit of a stream of dust left by a comet"

point in the sky. No matter in which part of the sky you see the meteor, trace back its path and it will cross that point.

Meteors which appear to have shorter paths will seem to be closer to the radiant because they are heading more directly towards you.

It's all down to perspective. The meteors are flying parallel to each other as they stream into the atmosphere, but their paths, when traced back, converge on their radiant just as the parallel lanes of a long highway appear to converge in the distance.

ABOVE: *Several meteors, some very faint, can be seen bursting across the sky in the last big Leonid meteor storm in 1999.*

Meteor showers appear to radiate from a single point.

the part of the Earth where the observer is situated is likely to be turning into the direction from which the meteors come. The combined speeds of the rotating Earth and the traveling meteor particle make any meteor travel faster and burn brighter.

Meteor observation is an ideal project for the stargazer who's starting out, because it's a fun activity to share with friends but can also be of genuine scientific value.

You will need a watch, a notebook, a red light and a writing implement. A voice recorder will help you to make your notes without taking your eyes off the sky. Find a spot well away from streetlights, sit for an hour or so at a time steadily watching one particular patch of sky, say half-way between the horizon and the zenith.

Individual showers are commonly named after the constellation in which the radiant appears to lie. So the strong shower that occurs every August and appears to radiate from the direction of Perseus is called the Perseid meteor shower, or simply the Perseids. Similarly, a major December shower radiating from Gemini is known as the Geminids. Some shower names even specify a bright star close to their radiants, such as the Delta Aquarids or Kappa Cygnids.

It's not only the brightness of the sky during a meteor shower that affects the numbers seen. Many radiants don't rise above the horizon until after midnight, and the higher the radiant is in the sky, the more meteors will be seen. Also, as we get closer to dawn,

A solitary Perseid meteor is captured in this image.

When a meteor appears, quickly note the time, estimate the meteor's approximate brightness compared to the stars, its color, relative speed (such as fast, medium or slow) and features, such as whether it left a train. Note, also, whether the meteor was a shower member or a sporadic. Observe the sky conditions such as the presence of haze, cloud or moonlight and the brightness of the faintest stars overhead. Collectively these are called the limiting magnitude.

Your observations could be very useful to astronomical organizations and professional meteor scientists when combined with other members' records.

Don't expect to see the number of meteors quoted for any shower's maximum rate. This is usually a figure applied in ideal conditions and with the shower's radiant directly overhead, and is called the Zenithal Hourly Rate, or ZHR.

A meteorite weighing 37kg recovered from Canyon Diablo, Arizona.

There are very rare occasions, called meteor storms, when observers witness great numbers of meteors. The storms happen when the Earth passes through a dense clump of particles in the stream's orbit.

The Leonids generally reveal just a handful of meteors at maximum in November, but many thousands an hour may be seen at intervals of around 33 years. The last spectacular display was in 1999.

The following is a selection of the main showers of the year, as compiled by the International Meteor Organization. Those radiating from constellations in the northern sky are best seen from the northern hemisphere and those from southern constellations from the southern hemisphere.

SHOWER	WHEN VISIBLE	DATE OF MAXIMUM	ZHR
Quadrantids	Jan 01 – Jan 05	Jan 04	120
Lyrids	Apr 16 – Apr 25	Apr 22	18
Eta-Aquarids	Apr 19 – May 28	May 06	60
South Delta-Aquarids	Jul 12 – Aug 19	Jul 28	20
Perseids	Jul 17 – Aug 24	Aug 13	100
Orionids	Oct 02 – Nov 07	Oct 21	23
Southern Taurids	Oct 01 – Nov 25	Nov 05	5
Northern Taurids	Oct 01 – Nov 25	Nov 12	5
Leonids	Nov 10 – Nov 23	Nov 18	15+
Puppid/Velids	Dec 01 – Dec 15	Dec 07	10
Geminids	Dec 07 – Dec 17	Dec 14	120
Ursids	Dec 17 – Dec 26	Dec 23	10

THE AURORA
AND OTHER SKYGLOWS

One of the brightest flares ever seen on the Sun, the first of a swift string of fiery eruptions, exploded into view on September 7, 2005. Three days later, the dramatic blasts made their effects felt on the Earth.

A tidal wave of highly charged particles buffeted the magnetic field which surrounds our planet, producing a major space weather storm.

This magnetosphere acted as a defensive shield, protecting us from being bombarded by massive doses of deadly radiation. But it also set the heavens ablaze, producing a brilliant and colorful light show in the night sky.

This phenomenon was a spectacular example of the aurora, a sky glow which occurs fairly frequently at high latitudes around the north and south magnetic poles. It is popularly known as the Northern or Southern Lights, depending on which hemisphere you live in, or the aurora borealis and aurora australis in scientific terms. It becomes a much rarer happening the further one travels from those poles.

The storm of September 2005 was so powerful, that the aurora was seen as far south as Arizona and the Mediterranean.

Most aurorae occur in the shape of pulsating or rippling glows, but there is a range of other forms which appear, including arcs and rays. The bigger storms create the classic curtains which fill the entire sky.

When observing, try to move away from streetlights and find a clear, dark sky to obtain the best display. The pulsations are subtle and moonlight may drown them. A great display can make for some spectacular photos; put your camera on a tripod and open the shutter for several seconds.

Because aurorae occur as a direct result of disturbances on the Sun, activity tends to be more frequent when the Sun is at the most active stage of its 11-year cycle. It remains unpredictable, though, and dramatic shows have been witnessed close to solar minimum.

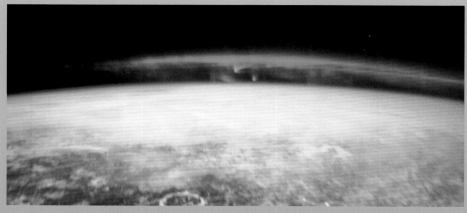

A unique view of the aurora, as seen from abve by astronauts orbiting the Earth aboard the International Space Station.

A classic view of a spectacular aurora, producing dancing curtains of light in the skies above a wintry landscape at a far northern latitude. This natural light show was sparked by the arrival of energetic particles from a storm on the Sun as they collided with the Earth's magnetic field.

Space scientists endeavor to learn more about the link between solar eruptions and aurorae because major storms threaten communications, power grids and satellite electronics and astronauts' lives.

ZODIACAL LIGHT

There are other glows in the sky worth observing for if you're lucky enough to have clear, dark skies and if moonlight is not a problem. They are not related to the aurora and are, instead, caused by dust spread through the solar system.

There are tiny, scattered specks of dust which combine to reflect the Sun's light back at us. This dust lies in the same plane as the planets' orbits, which passes through the zodiac, and is therefore known as the Zodiacal Light.

The glow appears particularly concentrated approaching the Sun and produces a ghostly cone in the sky before dawn or after sunset. It is best seen at times of the year when the ecliptic stands highest in the sky. Under ideal skies, such as in the tropics, it may be mistaken for the remains of twilight.

Even harder to spot is the Gegenschein, a large but ultra-faint glow found on the opposite side of the sky to the Sun. The clearest, darkest skies are necessary to see this phenomenon, which is again due to sunlight being reflected by distant dust.

MARVELS OF THE SKY
BEYOND THE SOLAR SYSTEM

The magnitude of space is difficult to grasp: Pluto lies so far away from Earth that its light takes around five and a half hours to reach us. The solar system may be two light years or more across.

A sense of the enormity of the universe is gained when you consider that one would travel for four and a half light-years through space before reaching the nearest star to the Sun. This distance, too, becomes insignificant against the scale of the Milky Way. Our home galaxy is made up of 200 billion or more stars within a pinwheel-shaped disk that stretches as much as 100,000 light years from one side to the other.

Of course, it doesn't end there. The Milky Way is just one of billions of galaxies, each filled with billions of stars, filling a visible universe more than 90 billion light years wide.

A snapshot of a tiny region of sky, taken by the Hubble space telescope is seen to contain 10,000 galaxies up to 13 billion light years away.

There is still much uncertainty about the true nature of the universe and whether it is part of a host of universes with other, as yet undiscovered dimensions. The evidence is that we may only be able to calculate a twentieth of the material that makes up our own universe. But let us look at some of the wonders of the universe that we know about.

THE STARS

Every star we see when we look up at the clear night sky is part of our own galaxy, the Milky Way. And although even the brightest appears as merely a pinprick of light, all of them are suns similar to our own. And the 2,000 or so visible to the naked eye are a fraction of the many billions in the galaxy.

Light from the outburst of the variable star V838 Monocerotis echoes from a cloud of surrounding gas in a view by the Hubble Space Telescope.

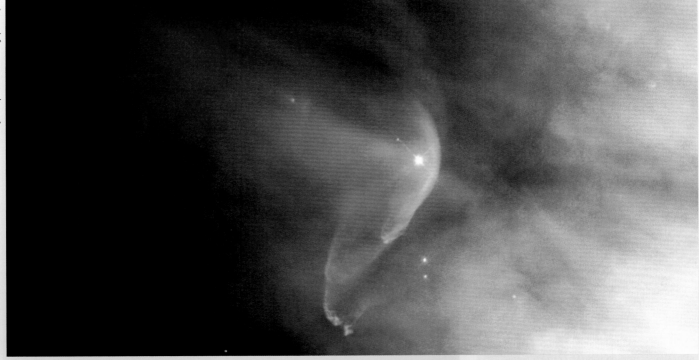

NASA Jet Propulsion Laboratory (NASA-JPL)

Astronomers using the Hubble have found a bow shock around a very young star in the Orion Nebula.

Stars come in many different shapes, sizes, colors and brightnesses, and these often indicate the stage they have reached in their own evolution.

Stars are born within huge swirling clouds of gas and dust. We can see the process happening today inside so-called celestial nurseries such as the famous Great Orion Nebula. A spinning disk of material condenses until a star forms at its center and shines by turning hydrogen into helium in a nuclear furnace. As the rest of the debris collects in orbit around the new star, other bodies, such as planets, are created.

Some stars are blue, condensed and super hot. Others nearing the end of their lives have become bloated red giants swollen hugely in size. Our Sun is middle-aged and will eventually meet such a fate itself, when it grows to a size including the orbit of Mars. By that time it will have had a life of around nine billion years. Eventually it will throw off a shell of material, and became what is called a planetary nebula.

Not all stars meet this relatively gentle demise. Some become so large and bright they explode as a supernova, making them – for a short while – as brilliant as all the other stars in a galaxy combined.

Stars are rated according to color and temperature. These basic "spectral types", beginning with the hottest, are O, B, A, F, G, K and M, with numbered subdivisions. Use the mnemonic Oh Be A Fine Girl, Kiss Me! The Sun is a G2 star on this scale.

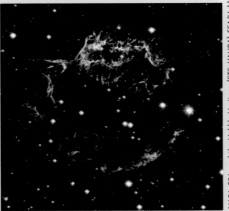

NASA, ESA, and the Hubble Heritage (STScI/AURA)-ESA/Hubble Collaboration

Hubble shot of the tattered remains of a star which exploded as a supernova in Cassiopeia.

> # "Astronomers are able to gauge the distances to stars, sizes, temperatures at which they burn and whether they have planets"

NASA Johnson Space Center – Earth

Hot blue stars have a much shorter lifespan.

It is remarkable that we can tell so much about stars. These days astronomers gauge their distances, sizes, temperatures at which they burn, whether they have planets and even what the atmospheres some of those planets contain. This has been arrived at by assembling the pieces of a puzzle scientists began to put together thousands of years ago.

Eratosthenes, the Greek scholar who lived around 200 years before Christ, set the ball rolling by defining the first measurement of the size of the Earth (he was also way ahead of his time in believing it to be round). He did so by measuring the height of the Sun in the sky from two locations about 500mi/ 800km apart in what is now Egypt.

Other Greek scientists, including Aristarchus, measured the distance of the Moon by observing and calculating angles during eclipses of the Moon and Sun. They went on to make a first stab at the Sun's distance and size too, but with less success. However, these first steps allowed successive astronomers to build on and refine their work, allowing us gradually to know the size and scale of the solar system.

Stars are a lot further away than anything else in the solar system, as calculated by ingenious astronomers who worked out their distances too. They began with stars which were relatively close.

Friedrich Bessel was first in 1838, when he accurately measured the distance to 61 Cygni. The same year, other astronomers gauged how far away Vega and Alpha Centauri are. They did so by using a technique called parallax, which you can use yourself very easily. Hold a finger up in front of your face, close one eye and note where the finger appears against the background. Now, without moving your finger, view with the other eye instead. Your finger will appear to have shifted.

Parallax showed how the nearby stars seemed to shift position against distant background stars. The astronomers made observations when the Earth was on opposite sides of the Sun in its orbit, equivalent to putting our eyes a very long way apart.

Another breakthrough in the 19th century came with the invention of a device called the Spectroscope. Attached to a telescope this split simple star light into its rainbow of colors, like a prism. Through this spectrum

A Hubble image of the Crab Nebula, a six light year wide remnant of a supernova that was seen to explode in 1054.

could be seen a pattern of bright and dark lines, a bit like the barcodes we now use today. These are the "fingerprints" of different elements or materials, such as sodium, inside the stars. So in a flash, quite literally, we could tell what individual stars were made of.

The position of the lines for the various elements remained the same relative to each other. However, the pattern shifted its position along the spectrum of colors according to whether the star was traveling toward us or away from us, and its speed.

This phenomenon, called the Doppler Effect, is similar to that which changes the pitch of a siren on an emergency vehicle depending on whether it is approaching us or receding. In astronomy, it is called the Red Shift, indicating that an object is moving away while a Blue Shift is coming toward us.

The stars do not all shine in as stable a way as the Sun. Many vary hugely in brightness over a relatively short timescale. One type of variable star, called a Cepheid, changes in a particularly precise way. What's more, astronomers found that the time it takes to vary, called its period, was directly linked to the star's actual luminosity.

This was a gift to astronomers. By comparing the apparent brightness of a Cepheid to its period, they could determine the distance. When giant telescopes detected Cepheids in other nearby galaxies, we could estimate distances for those, too.

Distances to the other planets are expressed in kilometers or miles that can unwieldy. It is around 250,000mi/385,000km to the Moon, for example, and approximately 93 million mi/ 150 million km to the Sun. Astronomers had to find more useful scales to describe such vast measurements to the stars.

One standard chosen was the Earth-Sun distance itself, which is termed one Astronomical Unit (AU). Another is the lightyear – not, as many seem to think, a measurement of time but the distance that light travels in one year at the velocity of 186,282mi/299,792km a second in a vacuum. A further popular unit used by professional scientists is called the parsec, which equals 3.26 light years. The Sun is a solitary star, but many more double stars exist than single ones, and there are plenty of other systems containing three or more suns. Many of these double or multiple star systems are wide enough apart for us to view their separate stars through the telescope as they orbit each other. Others are too close to split.

If the stars are orbiting edge on to our line of sight, eclipses occur and the starlight fades and then brightens again at regular intervals. These form another class of variable star, bright examples being Algol in Perseus and Beta Lyrae, both of which can be followed with the naked eye.

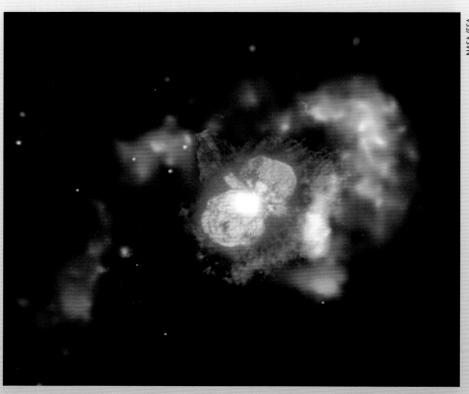

A huge, billowing pair of gas and dust clouds are captured in this stunning NASA Hubble Space Telescope image of the massive star Eta Carinae.

There are a number of different types of variable star, many of which are a lot less predictable than the Cepheids or eclipsing variables – and amateur astronomers can make a valuable contribution to science by monitoring them. The most spectacular type of variable star is the nova, a faint star which has suddenly undergone a huge, but non-destructive, explosion, temporarily becoming perhaps 10,000 times brighter.

The apparent brightness of stars is quoted by a measure called its magnitude. The brightest objects have negative magnitudes and each full magnitude is around two and a half times brighter than the next.

The brightest stars in the sky are around magnitude 1. The faintest visible with the naked eye in a dark sky is about magnitude 6. The Sun has a magnitude of -27. Stars are also given a second brightness rating, termed their absolute magnitude, which describes how they would really compare if they were all at a standard distance of 10 parsecs (32.6 light years).

The stars are not fixed in space but are moving through space. This change is generally only perceptible over many thousands of years, but it means the patterns in the sky will change with time. The Sun is moving too, traveling at around

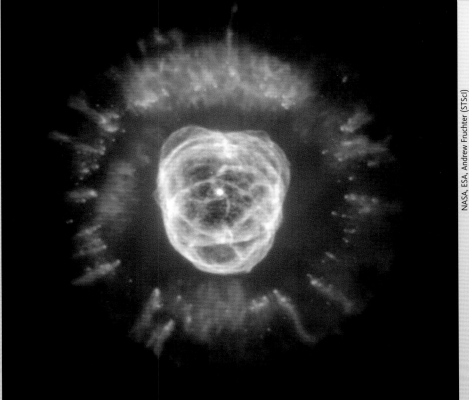

Away from light pollution, our own home galaxy, the Milky Way, can be seen as a glowing band with dark lanes of dust.

The Eskimo Nebula resembles a human face in a hood in this photo from Hubble. It is really a double shell of material ejected from a star that was once like the Sun but has died and become a planetary nebula. The Eskimo lies 5000 light years away in Gemini.

19mi/30km per second towards the bright star Vega.

The patterns we can see have been interpreted in different ways by civilizations around the world. Today there are officially 88 termed constellations, whose boundaries have been officially drawn by the International Astronomical Union.

We still call many of the brighter stars by names given them by Arabian astronomers many hundreds of years ago. And although there are modern, advanced catalogs, we also use the system started in 1603 of using the Greek alphabet to label the brighter stars, with the early letters usually, but not always, issued in order of brightness. Other stars have numbers from various other catalogs.

Stars are not arranged evenly across the sky. On a clear, dark night away from streetlights, it's not difficult to see the Milky Way stretching across the sky but our galaxy is widely spread but relatively thin.

The hazy band that we see is where stars are densest because we are looking edge-on through towards the center.

Though the term Milky Way was originally thought up to describe the band in the sky, we now use it to describe the galaxy itself. Determining the galaxy's shape is extremely difficult, but we know that the Milky Way is a spiral galaxy with arms of stars spreading outwards. The Sun is about two-thirds of the way out along one of these arms.

The age of the Milky Way has been estimated to be around 13.6 billion years – almost as old as the universe itself.

CLUSTERS, NEBULAE & GALAXIES

Point a pair of binoculars at the sky and it is relatively easy to detect that there are more than just stars and planets in the heavens. Many slightly fuzzy objects will catch your eye, especially if you sweep along areas of the Milky Way.

Closer inspection can reveal these blurred patches to be collections of faint stars. Others may continue to look fuzzy no matter how much you try to magnify them. These are the clusters and nebulae that are mainly to be found in our own galaxy and the myriad of other galaxies ranged across the universe.

For many years following the invention of the telescope, very little if anything was known about the true nature of most of these objects. Surprisingly, it was not until well into the 20th century that astronomers realized that some were other galaxies of stars outside our own Milky Way.

Astronomers decided early on that they served to confuse observation projects. The most famous index of the universe's indistinct inhabitants was drawn up by a French astronomer who was in the business of searching for comets sweeping the solar system.

"Charles Messier drew up a catalog of objects and their positions"

Charles Messier became frustrated when attempting to identify comets so, with the help of colleague Pierre Méchain, he drew

up an 18th century catalog of the blurred patches and their positions. In this way, comet-hunters had a reference guide to help them discount the imposters. There are 110 objects in Messier's list.

Today, Messier is better known for his famous catalog than for any of his comet discoveries. Amateur astronomers in particular still refer to the brightest clusters, nebulae and galaxies by their Messier or M numbers.

Later catalogues covered the vast number of objects Messier failed to include. The important ones for amateur observers include the New General Catalog of Nebulae and Clusters of Stars (NGC) of 1888 and its subsequent Index Catalog supplements (IC).

Europe's Gaia satellite will map a billion stars in the Milky Way after it launches in 2011.

©ESA

OPEN CLUSTERS

Some of the objects in Messier's catalog are clearly not comets.

The naked eye, for example, can tell that M45, the Pleiades or Seven Sisters, in Taurus is a collection of stars. Many other open clusters are further away and look more condensed and fuzzy through binoculars.

Some are much more spread out. The Hyades is another cluster in Taurus which does not have a Messier number because it forms a large and distinct V shape in the sky. More than 1,000 open clusters are known to exist.

The Milky Way stretching from Carina on the left to Orion on the right. Our satellite galaxy the Large Magellanic Cloud is seen lower left.

GLOBULAR CLUSTERS

If open clusters are scattered villages of stars, globular clusters are truly cosmic cities. These are huge, spherical concentrations of close-packed stars usually found in a wide halo around the galaxy. They are some of the oldest objects in the universe and many contain more than a million stars.

They can resemble the contents of an overturned sugar bowl and telescopes will often help pick out individual stars. Bright globular clusters include M13 in Hercules for northern observers and Omega Centauri for the southern hemisphere.

ESA/Hubble

Globular clusters are dense, spherical concentrations of many thousands, or sometimes millions, of stars and can often be found forming a wide halo around a galaxy. They are among the oldest objects found in the universe.

ESA ©2005 MPS for OSIRIS Team

This view of Mars (visible towards the top of the image) and of the Milky Way was taken by the OSRIS camera on board the Rosetta spaceprobe on December 3, 2006.

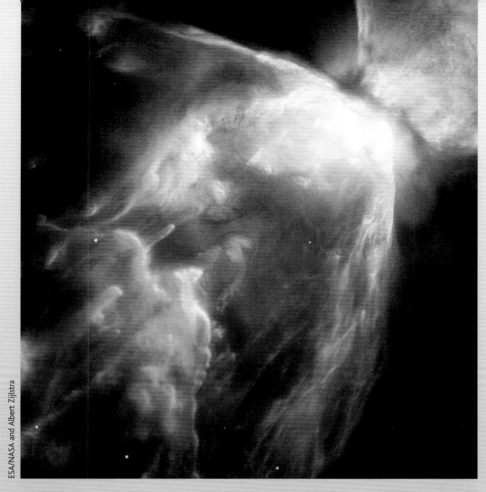

ESA/NASA and Albert Zijlstra

Beautiful images from the Hubble of the Butterfly Nebula in Scorpius, left, and Horsehead Nebula in Orion, below.

NEBULAE

Some fuzzy patches will remain unclear no matter how much you magnify them, because they are simply clouds of gas and dust. Mostly hydrogen, this gas may be a stellar birthplace, as in M42, the Orion Nebula. But it may also be the remains of a star's death in a catastrophic explosion. M1, the Crab Nebula in Taurus, is the tangled remains of just such a supernova that was seen to flare in 1054. So too is the Veil Nebula, the strands of gas from a much older blast.

Some gas clouds are known as emission nebulae because stars within them excite the gas and make it glow. Reflection nebulae are those that shine simply because they bounce back the light of nearby stars. A further type is the dark nebula, which makes itself visible as a silhouette obscuring bright regions behind it. The Coalsack in Crux and the Horsehead Nebula in Orion are examples.

Planetary nebulae are bright shells of gas thrown off by stars in their dying days. They were named for their shape and are totally unrelated to the planets, so the term can be misleading. Because the gas shell appears more concentrated at the edges, due to a line-of-sight effect, the spherical shell can look more like a ring. A classic case is M57, known as the Ring Nebula, in Lyra. A telescope may show the faint central star that shed its shell.

A Hubble view of the magnificent spiral galaxy NGC 4603, the most distant galaxy in which a special class of pulsating stars called Cepheid variables have been found.

GALAXIES

Ask someone to imagine a galaxy and they will probably produce a picture of a swirling spiral, with millions of stars sweeping away from its heart. This classic shape was first observed in the mid-19th century by the Third Earl of Rosse, using a telescope at Birr Castle, Ireland, (then the largest instrument in the world). Their real nature as vast collections of stars was then still unknown, so they were called spiral nebulae.

The Milky Way is a spiral galaxy. So too is our biggest neighbor, M31 in Andromeda, 2.5 million light years away, although it is hard to tell on first viewing as we are seeing it at an oblique angle. Other spirals, such as M51 and M101, are viewed from above, so their swirling patterns are clear. Still more, like NGC 891, which is also in Andromeda, are seen edge-on. They appear long and thin and the spiral pattern is completely hidden, but what is evident is the thicker bulge such galaxies have at their centers.

Such galaxies can be so huge that they contain many billions and sometimes even trillions of stars. Astronomers are finding that many, including the Milky Way, also contain a supermassive black hole at their heart, steadily devouring stars and other matter which swirls into its clutches.

Spiral galaxies vary in how tightly wound their arms are, and many also feature an elongated bar from which the arms coil. Our own galaxy is an example of a barred spiral.

Though spiral galaxies are common, they are not the only form a galaxy can take. So-called elliptical galaxies are conglomerations of stars which have oval forms but no structure within them. Irregular galaxies, more formless still, are believed to result from collisions, or close approaches, of two separate galaxies, or close approaches.

Some galaxies are described as being active because they have intensely hot, bright centers sending out enormous amounts of energy. These violent reactions are probably driven by the effects of the black holes at their centers. Powerful sources called quasars, which look like stars but emit as much energy as hordes of galaxies, are extreme examples of active galaxies.

Galaxies also have satellites of their own. The Milky Way has a number, including two irregular dwarf galaxies known as the Magellanic Clouds. Together with these, plus M31 and a number of others, the Milky Way is part of the so-called Local Group of galaxies.

This is not unusual. Most galaxies tend to collect together in clusters, which range in size from a few to many thousands. One notable large grouping is the Virgo Cluster, 60 million light years distant.

Observations of all galaxies outside our own Local Group reveal that they display a red shift when viewed through a spectroscope. This shows they are moving away from us and is key evidence that the universe is expanding following the Big Bang around 14 billion years ago.

VIEWING THE STARS

The stars shine all around us, in all directions. Which ones we see in our own sky depends on just where we live.

As we explained earlier, there are stars in the southern sky people living in northern latitudes never see, because they lie too far south. Inhabitants of the southern hemisphere cannot observe some of the stars of the northern hemisphere for the same reason. How much you see of the other hemisphere's stars depends on the latitude at which you live.

It is impossible to produce tailored sky maps for any particular night. The view changes from place to place. But we have found a three-stage solution.

First, we will present two maps, one showing the bright stars of the northern half of the celestial sphere and one displaying those

of the southern half. This is like separating the two halves of a globe and then printing each as a flat circular map. These two hemispheres, each bounded by the celestial equator, contain all 88 constellations, numbered in their alphabetical order along the bottom of the two pages.

If you live anywhere other than the areas around the North and South Poles, you will see, at some time during the year, the stars of your hemisphere plus a certain number of stars in the other hemisphere. If you live on the Equator, you will be lucky enough to see all the constellations in both hemispheres at some stage.

Our approach is also to create a few windows onto the sky. These are collections of star patterns, distinct during the late evening at different seasons in each hemisphere. We have also included a window for each of the areas of sky around the celestial poles, featuring constellations that you may either see every night or, if you live in the other hemisphere, never see at all.

The winter, spring, summer and autumn windows change due to the way, described earlier, that the stars appear to shift their positions in the sky, rising four minutes earlier every night. Because the Earth is turning, you will see more stars rising as the night wears on. Stay up into

The images shown here were all taken by Nik Szymanek with a CCD camera. The colors will not be visible to the naked eye.

M8 in Sagittarius

M16 in Serpens

the early hours and you will even get a sneak preview of the next season's sky window.

We are also presenting a rundown of all 88 of the constellations in the sky, including mentions of particularly interesting objects which you can observe within them, using binoculars or a small telescope. Many of these star patterns are fairly inconsequential, so we have picked 30 of the most prominent or interesting to illustrate with individual star maps.

You can still locate the others by using the two hemisphere charts, and if you want to see them all in detail, you could buy a dedicated star atlas or planetarium-type program for your computer.

Another useful tool is a star disk commonly called a Planisphere. You need to buy one that has been made for your home's approximate latitude. You then simply turn

it so that its oval window shows you the night sky as it appears for you at any time of the night on any date of the year.

The individual constellation maps in our book are drawn with north at the top. Depending on where you live or the time of night, you might see them the other way up or lying on their side.

The maps are marked with symbols to indicate objects mentioned in the text, whether stars, nebulae or star clusters.

All our targets are visible in amateur instruments if you pick a clear, dark night and are away from city lights.

> "If you live on the Equator, you will be lucky enough to see all the constellations from both hemispheres at some stage."

THE GREEK ALPHABET

The brighter stars in each constellation are usually indicated by a Greek letter. This table will help you match each Greek letter with its English spelling as used in the text:

α	Alpha	ν	Nu
β	Beta	ξ	Xi
γ	Gamma	ο	Omicron
δ	Delta	π	Pi
ε	Epsilon	ρ	Rho
ζ	Zeta	σ	Sigma
η	Eta	τ	Tau
θ	Theta	υ	Upsilon
ι	Iota	φ	Phi
κ	Kappa	χ	Chi
λ	Lambda	ψ	Psi
μ	Mu	ω	Omega

M31 in Andromeda

Orion Nebula M42 in Orion

NORTHERN HEMISPHERE

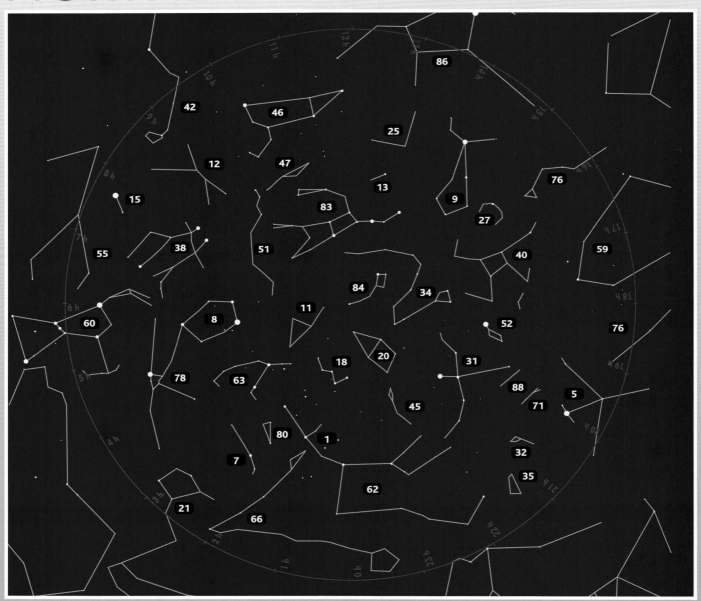

The 88 Constellations (numbered for charts).

1. Andromeda 2. Antlia 3. Apus 4. Aquarius 5. Aquila 6. Ara 7. Aries 8. Auriga 9. Boötes 10. Caelum 11. Camelopardalis 12. Cancer 13. Canes Venatici 14. Canis Major 15. Canis Minor
Borealis 28. Corvus 29. Crater 30. Crux 31. Cygnus 32. Delphinus 33. Dorado 34. Draco 35. Equuleus 36. Eridanus 37. Fornax 38. Gemini 39. Grus 40. Hercules 41. Horologium
Norma 58. Octans 59. Ophiuchus 60. Orion 61. Pavo 62. Pegasus 63. Perseus 64. Phoenix 65. Pictor 66. Pisces 67. Piscis Austrinus 68. Puppis 69. Pyxis 70. Reticulum 71. Sagitta
Ursa Minor 85. Vela 86. Virgo 87. Volans 88. Vulpecula

SOUTHERN HEMISPHERE

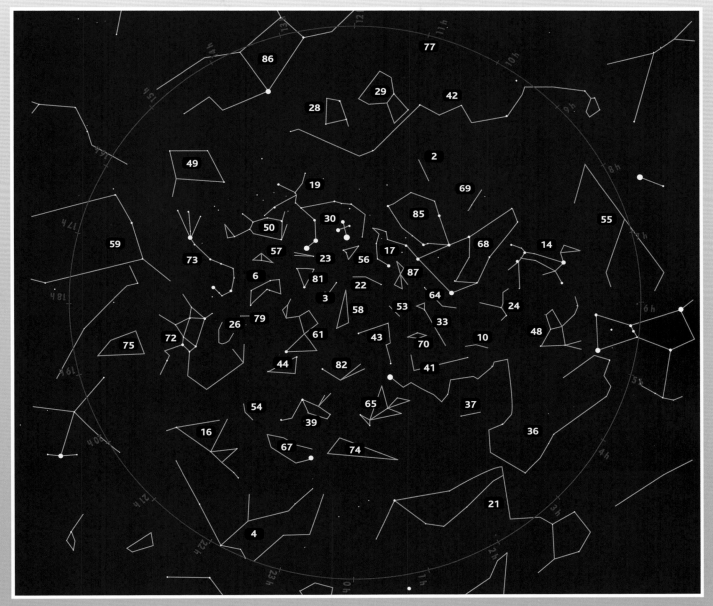

16. Capricornus 17. Carina 18. Cassiopeia 19. Centaurus 20. Cepheus 21. Cetus 22. Chamaeleon 23. Circinus 24. Columba 25. Coma Berenices 26. Corona Australis 27. Corona
42. Hydra 43. Hydrus 44. Indus 45. Lacerta 46. Leo 47. Leo Minor 48. Lepus 49. Libra 50. Lupus 51. Lynx 52. Lyra 53. Mensa 54. Microscopium 55. Monoceros 56. Musca 57.
72. Sagittarius 73. Scorpius 74. Sculptor 75. Scutum 76. Serpens 77. Sextans 78. Taurus 79. Telescopium 80. Triangulum 81. Triangulum Australe 82. Tucana 83. Ursa Major 84.

WINTER SKY WINDOW

DECEMBER TO FEBRUARY

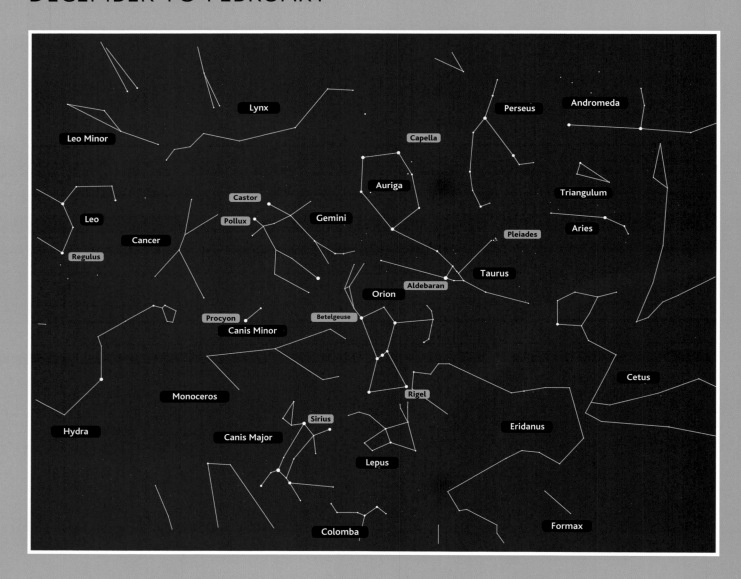

This window on the sky shows the general view looking south from the northern hemisphere. The bottom of the map approximates to your horizon and the constellation of Auriga lies more or less overhead during winter evenings. Winter is a good time to enjoy astronomy because the nights are long. As long as you wrap up warm, there are plenty of fine sights to enjoy.

WHAT TO SEE

The view south at this time is dominated by the magnificent constellation of Orion the hunter. And you can use this prominent constellation to help find other sky patterns.

Orion is easy to spot thanks to its line of three bright stars that make up the hunter's belt.

Above them, two bright stars mark Orion's shoulders, and below the belt, two others represent his knees. The top left star is Betelgeuse, a red supergiant. The color is fairly obvious to the eye.

Betelgeuse is 800 times the diameter of the Sun and 40,000 times brighter. It is considered a candidate for a supernova that will one day flare brilliantly in the sky before collapsing into a black hole. Betelgeuse lies 420 light years away.

The star at bottom right of Orion is Rigel, a hot blue superstar. Rigel is 60,000 times brighter than the Sun but nearly twice as far away as Betelgeuse, at a distance of 800 light years.

Follow the line of Orion's belt down to the left. The bright twinkling star is Sirius, the dog star, the brightest star in the night sky.

Sirius's brilliance is due entirely to the fact that it lies only eight light years away from Earth. It would look considerably fainter if it was as far away as Betelgeuse or Rigel.

Look above Sirius and to the left of Orion to find Procyon, a prominent star in an indistinct constellation called Canis Minor. Sirius, Procyon and Betelgeuse make up a clear Winter Triangle.

Look above Procyon to find two bright stars close together in the constellation of Gemini.

These are the twins Castor and Pollux. The upper twin is Castor and the lower is Pollux, viewed from the north.

Gemini is also the constellation from which one of the year's major meteor showers appears to radiate. Watch a clear, dark sky around December 13 and you may well see one or two bright meteors streaking across the heavens.

> "Orion is easy to spot because of its line of three bright stars"

We return to Orion's belt to find our next major constellation. Continue the line of three stars to the upper right and you come to a bright orange/red star called Aldebaran. This marks the eye of Taurus the Bull. It sits at one end of a large "V" shape of stars which form the Hyades star cluster. Aldebaran is not actually part of the cluster; it simply lies between the cluster and us.

SPRING SKY WINDOW

MARCH TO MAY

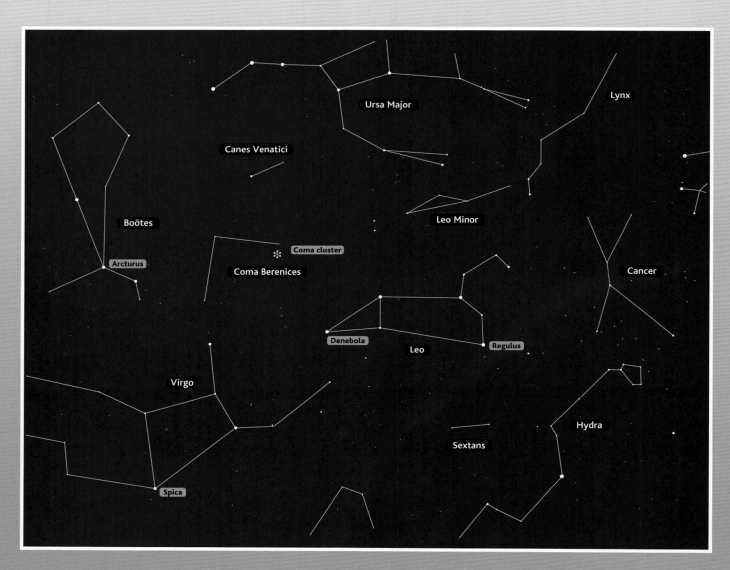

THE VIEW

This shows the general view looking south from the northern hemisphere which in spring, in the south, is dominated by Leo.

The bottom of the map approximates to your horizon and the constellation of Ursa Major lies roughly overhead during spring evenings.

WHAT TO SEE

Spring evening skies are dominated in the south by the Zodiacal constellation of Leo, the lion.

The head of the lion, resembling a giant question mark written backwards in the sky, is easy to spot. At the base of this hook is Regulus, the brightest star in Leo. This regal name, which literally means King Star, was awarded because the planets pass close by during their orbits of the Sun.

One passing through in 2008 and 2009 will be the bright ringed world Saturn, which will make Leo look as if it has gained an extra star.

Regulus is 150 times brighter than our Sun and 80 light years away. To its left, the triangle of stars which make up the haunches of the lion and his tail is marked by a star called Denebola.

Almost overhead is the Plough, a saucepan shape of seven stars within the constellation of Ursa Major. Some people call it the Big Dipper because it resembles a spoon.

Follow the curve of the spoon's handle down to the left until you come to Arcturus, the fourth brightest star in the sky. Arcturus, which is about 40 light years from Earth, is a red giant, nearing the end of its life.

Arcturus is the main star in the constellation of Boötes the Herdsman. Above it, you will see the kite-shape of stars that it consists of.

Look between Boötes and Leo to find a less distinct grouping of faint stars called Coma Berenices. This is worth seeking out because it contains a cascade of faint stars that are part of a star cluster called Coma.

You will need clear, dark skies to see them and they will appear more distinct if you look slightly away and view them out of the corner of your eye. This is a technique called averted vision and uses the fact that the human eye's receptors are more sensitive away from the center.

Continue the curved line that took you from the Plough to Arcturus and you will come to another bright star, Spica.

"Use 'averted vision' — when you view out of the corner of your eye — to see clusters better"

This is a super-luminous star, shining 14,000 times brighter than the Sun.

Spica is the brightest star in Virgo and lies 260 light years away from Earth. Virgo is another constellation of the Zodiac and Saturn moves into it in 2010 and 2011.

Virgo is famous for being home to a vast cluster of galaxies that lies an average distance of 60 million light years away from us. The cluster is so extensive that our own local group of galaxies, including the Milky Way and M31 in Andromeda, are actually related to it.

SUMMER SKY WINDOW

JUNE TO AUGUST

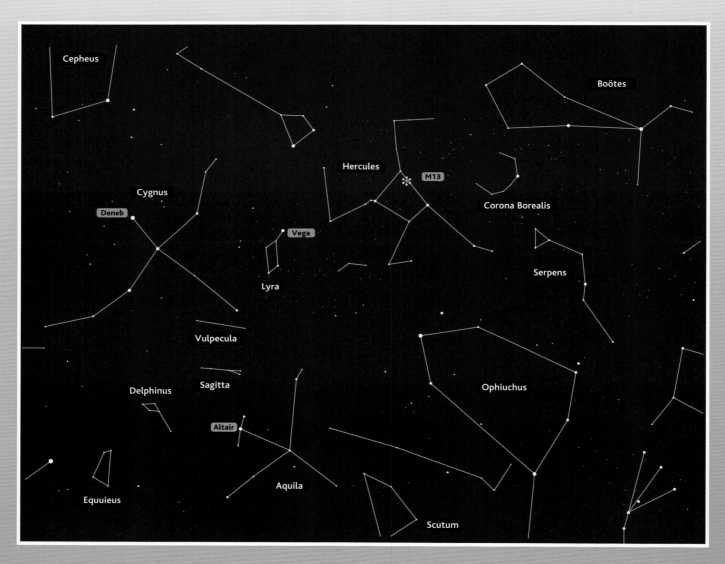

Cepheus

Boötes

Hercules

M13

Cygnus

Corona Borealis

Deneb

Vega

Serpens

Lyra

Vulpecula

Ophiuchus

Sagitta

Delphinus

Altair

Equuieus

Aquila

Scutum

THE VIEW

This window on the sky shows the general view looking south from the northern hemisphere in summer, when skies become darker much later in the evening and the nights are short.

WHAT TO SEE

When night does fall in the summer in the northern hemisphere three bright stars forming a prominent triangle are among the first to appear in the fading light.

These are Altair, Deneb and Vega, the brightest stars in Aquila, Cygnus and Lyra respectively. The unofficial pattern that they form is called the Summer Triangle. At top right in the triangle is Vega, the brightest of the three, largely because it is very close by astronomical standards – only 25 light years away.

Left of Vega is a genuinely brilliant star, Deneb. Although it appears fainter, it is really shining 70,000 times brighter than the Sun, but from a distance of 1,800 light years.

The third star of the triangle, Altair, is below the other two and is another whose brightness is mainly due to its distance. Altair is only ten times brighter than the Sun, but it lies even closer to us than Vega, being just 16 light years away. Two slightly fainter stars, one on either side of Altair, make it easy to identify.

Return to Deneb and look at a pattern of other stars which stretch from it into the Summer Triangle. These form the shape of a cross and represent the body of the flying swan that is the constellation of Cygnus. Deneb is at the tail end and the opposite end of the cross marks the bird's long neck. The middle struts indicate the swan's wings.

Because of its distinct shape, Cygnus is sometimes also known as the Northern Cross.

A couple of small but attractive groupings can also be found nearby. Below Cygnus, Sagitta resembles the Archer's arrow being shot into heaven. And to the left of Altair, you can see a tiny diamond of stars, with another star underneath. This is Delphinus the Dolphin, so named because it is as if it were leaping out of the sea.

Look to the right of Vega to identify another of the characters of the sky, the legendary hero Hercules. Although the stars that mark his body are not terribly bright, they form a distinctive enough pattern.

Find the two stars defining the right hand side of Hercules' torso. About a third of the way between them, from the top, can be seen one of the finest globular star clusters in the sky, M13. If there are really clear, dark skies, you might just be able to see it with the naked eye. Binoculars will show it as a fuzzy glow and it takes a telescope to display it as it really is – a tightly condensed ball of stars.

There are around one million stars packed together in this cluster, which lies about 25,000 light years away.

During 2008 and 2009, the great planet Jupiter will be low in the south during summer. If you are watching the area during the first couple of weeks in August in both years, you may catch a number of shooting stars. They are most likely to be members of the Perseid meteor shower, which peaks around August 12, although there are other showers active during the summer too.

AUTUMN SKY WINDOW

SEPTEMBER TO NOVEMBER

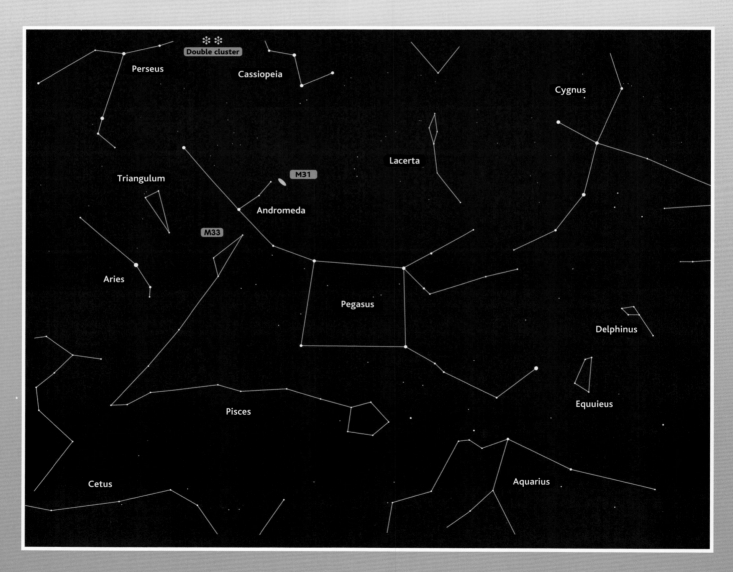

THE VIEW

This window on the sky shows the general view looking south from the northern hemisphere in autumn. The bottom of the map approximates to your horizon and the 'W' shape of Cassiopeia should be overhead

WHAT TO SEE

For northern observers, nights draw out once more at this time, presenting the chance to start observing the sky earlier in the evening.

As it darkens, you will see the stars of Cygnus, now flying further to the west. To their left, in an otherwise fairly barren region of the sky, you should be able to make out a giant square of four stars.

None is particularly bright, but this shape, dubbed the Great Square of Pegasus, is a distinctive one, although the top left star is actually borrowed from neighboring constellation Andromeda.

From the bottom right star in the square, more stars stretch to make the neck and head of Pegasus, the winged horse, revealing that it is actually flying upside down.

Return to the top left star in the square, and look for a line of stars stretching away to the upper left. These mark Andromeda (The Princess).

Two stars along, another pair of stars branch off upwards. Look here for the closest giant galaxy outside our own Milky Way, known as M31 or the Great Andromeda Galaxy.

M31 is fairly easy to spot with the naked eye as a large hazy blob, if you have a clear, dark sky and stand away from streetlights. But as it lies an incredible distance of 2.5 million light years away, it is probably the furthest object that most of us will see with our eyes alone. Its light that we see today left the galaxy before Man inhabited the Earth.

Binoculars or a small telescope will show the fuzzy, elongated blur of the galaxy more clearly. Below Andromeda is a small triangle of stars called, fittingly, Triangulum.

In this constellation lies the galaxy M33, which binoculars will pick out in clear skies.

Legend has it that Andromeda was rescued from a sea monster, which still lurks nearby in the sky. Cetus, also known as the Whale, can be found by following a line from the top right star in the square of Pegasus through the bottom left star.

Between Pegasus and Cetus is a long V-pattern of stars representing Pisces, the two fish of the Zodiac. A bright new "star" will travel through this faint star pattern between 2010 and 2012 – the giant planet Jupiter.

Return to Andromeda and extend its main line of stars away from Pegasus and you will reach another celestial hero – Perseus.

Above Andromeda, and roughly overhead on autumn evenings, is the "W" shape of Cassiopeia. Look between Perseus and the W with binoculars and you will spot two attractive concentrations of stars. These form the famous Double Cluster, NGC 884 and NGC 869.

These lie around 8,000 light years away. Through a small telescope they look like collections of sparkling jewels.

SKY WINDOW

ALL YEAR STARS

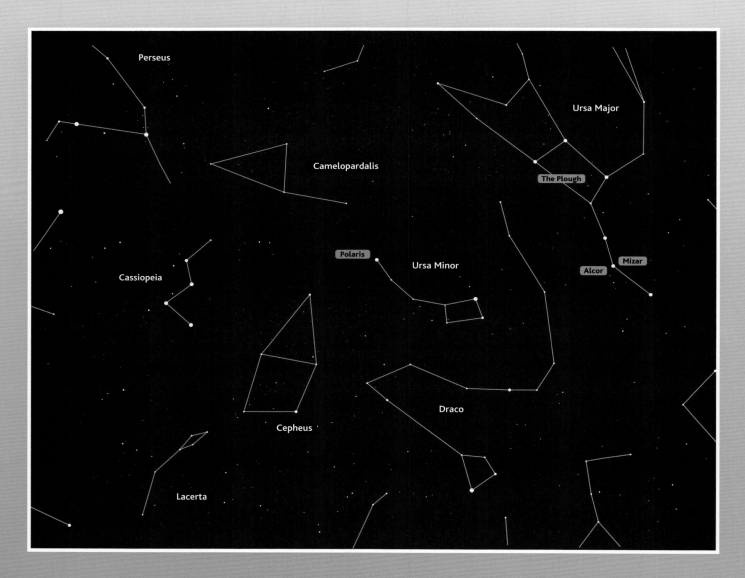

Perseus

Camelopardalis

Ursa Major

The Plough

Cassiopeia

Polaris

Ursa Minor

Mizar

Alcor

Cepheus

Draco

Lacerta

THE VIEW

Previous sky windows have shown us the views looking south at different seasons of the year. For our final window for the northern hemisphere, you need to turn and face in the opposite direction, due north.

WHAT TO SEE

When you look north, you see the patterns of stars that lie close to the North Celestial Pole. Helpfully, this point in the sky is marked by a fairly bright star called Polaris.

Throughout the night and, indeed, throughout the year, the other constellations in our window appear to wheel around Polaris as the Earth rotates. But those stars closer to Polaris than the horizon never set and remain visible at any time. They are described as circumpolar.

This means that, whatever season it is, the patterns on view in this direction remain the same, although their position changes, just like the hands of a clock.

How many stars are circumpolar depends on the latitude at which you live. The view here shows these northern stars as they appear on a mid-evening in spring.

The well-known pattern of the Plough, or Big Dipper, in Ursa Major, the Great Bear, is climbing in the sky to the right, with its top two stars, dubbed the Pointers, doing just that – pointing to Polaris in Ursa Minor.

The stars of Ursa Minor itself, sometimes dubbed the Little Dipper, curve away from Polaris toward the handle of the Plough.

Look to the other side of Polaris from the Plough and you will find the distinctive "W" shape of Cassiopeia, the queen. In this view, Cassiopeia is seen on its side and slowly sinking, like the hands of a clock running backwards. This view revolves, counterclockwise around Polaris as the night wears on.

If you view this direction on a summer evening, the Plough will lie at the top of the map, virtually overhead, while Cassiopeia will resemble that "W" low above the northern horizon.

On autumn evenings, the Plough will be descending again on the left hand side of the sky window with Cassiopeia rising on the right side. And at the same time in winter, it will be the Plough that is low in the north and Cassiopeia that lies overhead.

Look at the second star from the end of the handle of the Plough with the naked eye and you will see that it has another close by.

The brighter star is called Mizar and the fainter is Alcor. A telescope shows that Mizar is a close double star itself.

Between Ursa Major and Ursa Minor, a straggly line of stars forms the tail of Draco, the dragon. Follow the meandering line to locate the diamond shape marking the dragon's head.

Look between the head of Draco and Cassiopeia and you will find Cepheus, a constellation representing Cassiopeia's husband, the King. The house-like shape is not bright but it is not too difficult to make out.

"Cassiopeia slowly sinks like the hands of a clock running backwards"

SUMMER SKY WINDOW

DECEMBER TO FEBRUARY

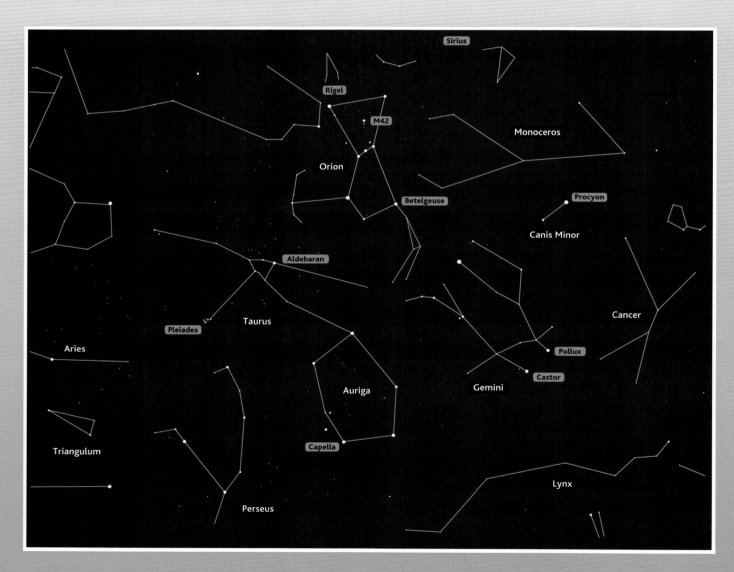

THE VIEW

This window on the sky shows the general view looking north from the southern hemisphere. The bottom of the map approximates to your horizon.

To help get your bearings, use a use a compass to find north or stand with the direction of sunset, in the west to your left. For example, changing south to north and right to left.

WHAT TO SEE

The view south at this time is dominated by the magnificent constellation of Orion the hunter. You can use this prominent constellation to help find other sky patterns.

Orion is easy to spot thanks to its line of the three bright stars that make up the hunter's belt. But from the southern hemisphere, the hunter is standing upside down.

Below the belt, two bright stars mark Orion's his knees. The bottom right star is Betelgeuse, a red supergiant whose color is fairly obvious to the eye.

Betelgeuse is 800 times the diameter of the Sun and 40,000 times brighter. Lying 420 light years away, it is considered a candidate for a supernova which will one day flare brilliantly in the sky before collapsing into a black hole.

The star at top left is Rigel, a hot blue superstar. Rigel is 60,000 times brighter than the Sun but nearly twice as far away as Betelgeuse, at a distance of 800 light years.

Follow the line of Orion's belt up to the right. The bright twinkling star is the brightest star in our night sky: Sirius, the dog star. Sirius's great brilliance is due entirely to the fact that it lies only eight light years away from Earth.

It would look considerably fainter if you put it as far away as Betelgeuse or Rigel.

Look below Sirius and to the right of Orion to find the next bright star in our sky window. This is Procyon, a prominent star in an indistinct constellation called Canis Minor. Sirius, Procyon and Betelgeuse make up a clear triangle.

Look below Procyon to find two bright stars close together in the constellation of Gemini. These are the twins Castor and Pollux. The lower twin is Castor and the upper is Pollux, viewed from the south.

Gemini is also the constellation from which one of the year's major meteor showers appears to radiate. Watch a clear dark sky around December 13 and you may see one or two bright meteors streaking across the heavens.

We return to Orion's belt to find our next major constellation. Continue the line of three stars down to the lower left and you will soon come to a bright orange/red star called Aldebaran, which marks the eye of Taurus the bull. You can see that it sits at one end of a large "V" shape of stars, which form the Hyades star cluster. Aldebaran is not really part of the cluster; it simply lies between the cluster and us.

Continue the line from Orion's belt through Aldebaran and you come to another pretty little cluster of stars, which the poet Tennyson compared to "a swarm of fireflies". These are the Pleiades, popularly known as the Seven Sisters because a keen-sighted observer can see seven with the naked eye.

Most people will be lucky to spot six, but a telescope will reveal hundreds of stars in this cluster.

Low in the sky you might see a very bright yellow star, Capella, in the constellation of Auriga the chariot driver. Capella is the 11th brightest star in the sky and lies 42 light years away. Its light actually shines from a pair of stars so close together that the naked eye cannot separate them.

AUTUMN SKY WINDOW

MARCH TO MAY

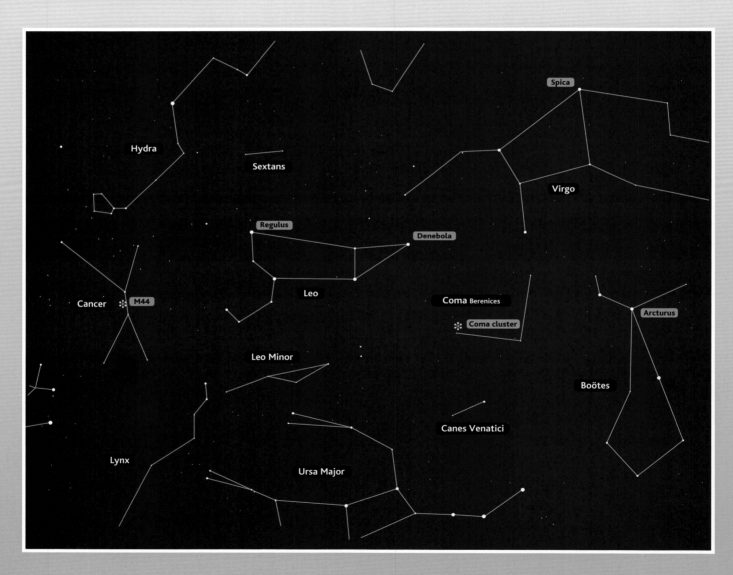

This shows the general view looking north from the southern hemisphere. The bottom of the map approximates to your horizon.

To help get your bearings, use a use a compass to find north or stand with the direction of sunset, in the west to your left. For example, changing south to north and right to left.

WHAT TO SEE

Spring evening skies are dominated in the north by the Zodiacal constellation of Leo, the lion.

The head of the lion is easy to spot, resembling as it does a giant upside-down question mark written backwards in the sky. At the top of this hook is the brightest star in Leo, Regulus. This regal name, literally meaning King Star, was awarded because the planets pass close by during their orbits of the Sun.

One passing through in 2008 and 2009 is the bright ringed world Saturn, which will make Leo look as if it has gained an extra star.

Regulus is 150 times brighter than our Sun and 80 light years away. To its right, a triangle of stars makes up the haunches of the lion and the tail is marked by a star called Denebola.

Look further to the right and you will come to a bright star called Arcturus. This, the fourth brightest star in the sky, is a red giant, nearing the end of its life, about 40 light years from Earth.

Arcturus is the main star in the constellation of Boötes, the Herdsman. The kite-shape of stars that make up this figure can be seen stretching below it.

Look between Boötes and Leo to find a less distinct grouping of faint stars called Coma Berenices. It is worth seeking out because it contains a cascade of faint stars that are part of a star cluster called Coma.

You will need clear dark skies to see them and they will appear more distinct if you look slightly away and view them out of the corner of your eye. This is a technique called averted vision and uses the fact that the human eye's receptors are more sensitive away from the center.

Look above Coma to find bright Spica, a super-luminous star, shining 14,000 times brighter than the Sun.

Spica is the brightest star in Virgo and lies 260 light years away from Earth. Virgo is another constellation of the Zodiac, and Saturn moves into it in 2010 and 2011.

Virgo is famous for being home to a vast cluster of galaxies that lies an average distance of 60 million light years away. The cluster is so extensive that our own local group of galaxies, including the Milky Way and M31 in Andromeda, are actually related to it.

"Saturn will make Leo look like it has gained an extra star"

WINTER SKY WINDOW

JUNE TO AUGUST

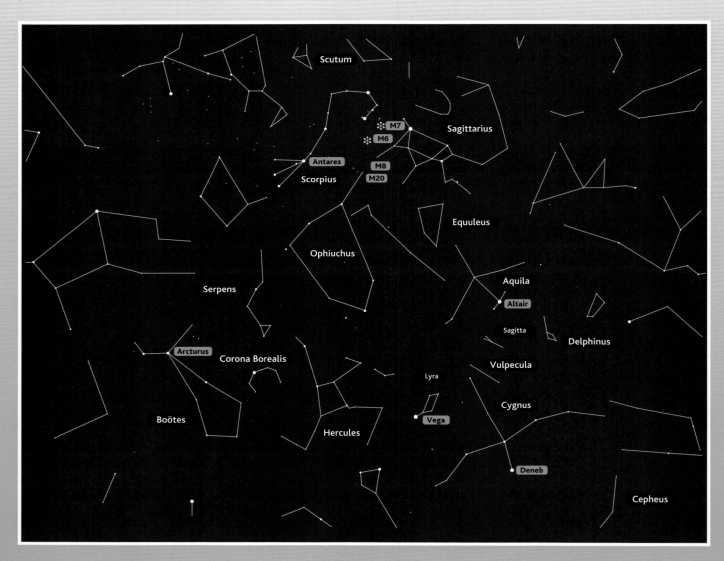

THE VIEW

This window on the sky shows the general view looking north from the southern hemisphere in winter, when longer nights offer up some of the finest sights.

WHAT TO SEE

Among the sights viewable during the longer nights of southern winter are the treasures of the Milky Way.

Look high in the sky to find the distinctive shape of Scorpius, the scorpion that legend has it killed Orion with its sting.

Its brightest star is the red giant Antares, whose name literally means rival of Mars. It was so named because its color means it can be confused for the Red Planet when Mars arrives close by on its journey through the Zodiac.

> ## "If there are dark skies you have the richest views of the Milky Way"

Follow the curve of the scorpion's body upwards and you can see the stars which represent its poisonous sting. Below Antares, more stars form the creature's claws.

Look to the right of Scorpius for another Zodiacal constellation, Sagittarius the Archer. You might find it easier to spot a more mundane image in these stars: the Teapot. Four stars form the pot, two stars to the right make his handle and another to the left completes his spout.

If there are dark skies, you will have the richest views of the Milky Way in Sagittarius, because you are looking towards the heart of the galaxy. The center itself is hidden by clouds of dust and gas, but we see stars densely packed.

Some of the greatest star clusters and nebulae are to be found in this region of the Milky Way, making it a delight to sweep with binoculars or a small telescope.

Below the teapot are two nebulae called M8 (the Lagoon), which is one of the brightest gas clouds in the sky, and M20 (the Trifid Nebula), which is somewhat dimmer.

Above these nebulae are two magnificent star clusters: M7 (called Ptolemy's Cluster) and, below and to its left, M6, the Butterfly

> ## "Legend has it that Scorpius the Scorpion killed Orion with its sting"

Cluster. M6 and M7 each contain around 130 stars and are best seen through binoculars.

Below Scorpius, a large, faint pattern of stars makes up Ophiuchus, the serpent holder. You can find the snake he carries in the two halves of Serpens on either side of him.

Below Ophiuchus, you may spot the mythical hero Hercules, with the brilliant star Vega low in the sky to the right. It is bright because it lies only 25 light years away.

During 2008 and 2009, Jupiter will be a prominent visitor to this sky window, standing high in the sky.

SPRING SKY WINDOW

SEPTEMBER TO NOVEMBER

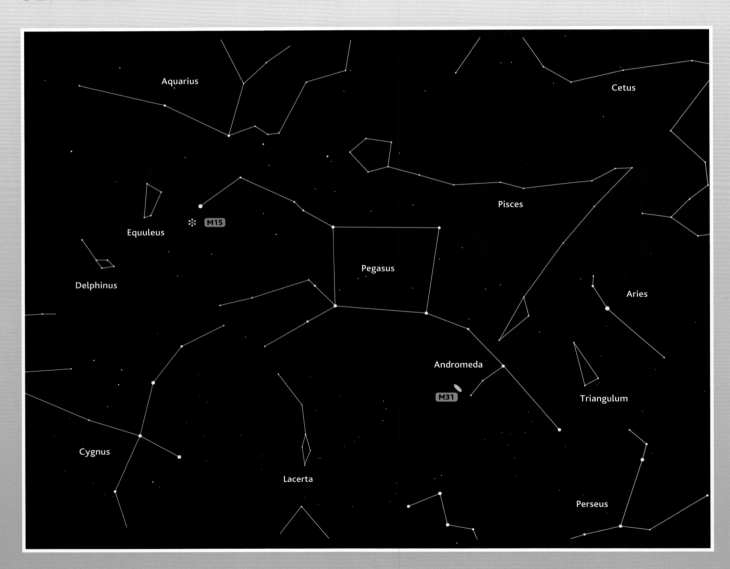

This window on the sky shows the general view looking north from the southern hemisphere in spring. The bottom of the map approximates to your horizon and the view north is dominated by four stars.

WHAT TO SEE

The prominent square of four medium-bright stars is the famous Great Square of Pegasus, part of the mythological winged horse, and a constellation that southern observers will see the right way up.

The square forms the horse's body and a curved line of stars runs from top left to produce his head. More stars from the base of the square make up his front legs.

Just to the left of the head, binoculars will reveal what first appears as a rather fuzzy star. This is actually a fine globular cluster of tightly packed stars called M15, and makes an excellent target for small telescopes.

Technically, the star at bottom right of the Great Square does not belong to Pegasus at all. It has been borrowed from the neighboring constellation of Andromeda, the princess.

The stars of Andromeda stretch away to the lower right. Two bright stars along, another pair of stars branch off downwards. Look here to spot the closest giant galaxy outside our own Milky Way, known as M31 or the Great Andromeda Galaxy.

Although M31 does not get very high from southern locations, you may be able to spot it as a large hazy blob with the naked eye if you have a clear, dark sky and stand away from streetlights. Since it lies an incredible distance of 2.5 million light years away, it is probably the furthest object most of us will see with our eyes alone. As we know, the light that we see today from this galaxy left it before Man inhabited the Earth.

Binoculars or a small telescope will show the fuzzy, elongated blur of the galaxy more clearly.

Above Andromeda lies the compact triangle of stars called Triangulum. In this constellation another nearby spiral galaxy, M33, can be picked out in binoculars in clear skies.

Cetus, also known as the whale, can be found by following a line from the bottom left star in the Square of Pegasus through the top right star.

Between Pegasus and Cetus is a long "V" pattern of stars that represents Pisces, the two fish of the Zodiac. A bright new "star" will travel through this faint star pattern between 2010 and 2012 – the giant planet Jupiter.

Return to the head of Pegasus and look above it to find the stars of Zodiacal constellation Aquarius, the Water Carrier. To the left of Pegasus is an attractive, tiny diamond shape of stars: Delphinus, the dolphin. Another star running above the diamond is the dolphin's tail.

None of the stars in this watery region of the sky is particularly bright but they will receive a particularly brilliant visitor when Jupiter passes through.

"Jupiter will travel between Pegasus and Cetus between 2010 and 2012"

SKY WINDOW

ALL YEAR STARS

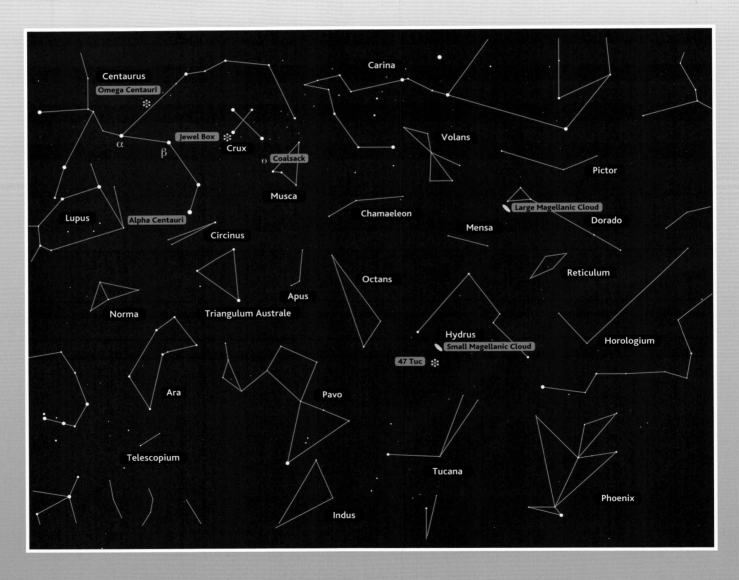

THE VIEW

Previous sky windows have shown us the views looking north at different seasons of the year. For our final window for the southern hemisphere, you need to turn and face in the opposite direction, due south.

WHAT TO SEE

When you look south, you see the patterns of stars that lie close to the South Celestial Pole. Unfortunately, there is no bright star to mark this point in the sky as there is for the northern pole, but we we can help you locate it.

Throughout the night and throughout the year, the other constellations in our window appear to wheel around the South Celestial Pole as the Earth rotates. But those stars closer to the pole than the horizon never set and remain visible at any time. They are said to be circumpolar.

The view here shows these southern stars as they appear on a mid-evening during autumn in the southern hemisphere.

The best known star sign is Crux, the Southern Cross, which is rising at this time as it circles the pole in a clockwise direction. Six months later at this time, Crux will be sinking low on the opposite side of the pole.

The point where the Celestial Pole lies is in Octans, just above the letter "t" in the word "Octans" in our sky window. One way to find it is to follow the long bar of the Southern Cross which points to it. Follow the bar by

around four and a half times its length and you will be there.

Crux contains a cluster of stars called the Jewel Box plus a dark patch in the sky, which is really a cloud of dust called the Coalsack.

Below Crux at this time can be found two bright stars: Alpha and Beta in Centaurus. In fact they point to the Southern Cross and so can also help you to find it. Alpha is the star further from the cross and is part of the closest star system to us. Its small red dwarf companion, Proxima Centauri, is the nearest star after the Sun, and lies just 4.2 light years away.

Also in Centaurus, close to Crux, can be found Omega Centauri, the finest globular star cluster in the entire sky. A fuzzy glow to the naked eye, it appears as a grainy ball in binoculars. A small telescope shows countless stars packed together.

On a clear, dark night, two wispy star clouds are visible in this window on the sky. These are the Magellanic Clouds. They are dwarf satellite galaxies of our own Milky Way, lying around 160,000 light years away and 75,000

light years apart.

The Magellanic Clouds form an equilateral triangle with the South Celestial Pole, offering another way to locate this.

Close to the Small Magellanic Cloud (SMC) can be found another spectacular globular cluster in Tucana, called 47 Tucanae or simply 47 Tuc. It appears as a fuzzy star with the naked eye and lies about 13,000 light years away.

"Find Octans by following the long bar of the Southern Cross"

ANDROMEDA

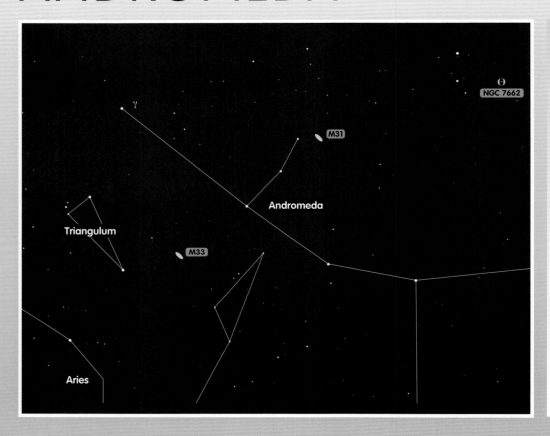

γ

NGC 7662

M31

Andromeda

Triangulum

M33

Aries

ANTLIA

This is one of the "modern" constellations, lying too far south in the sky to have been noticed by the ancient civilizations of the north. Its name, awarded by French astronomer Nicolas Louis de Lacaille in 1751-52, means the Air Pump.

Antlia contains little of interest other than Zeta, a widely-spaced pair of 6th magnitude stars for binoculars, and NGC 3132, a bright planetary nebula for small telescopes.

This constellation is named after a legendary Ethiopian princess who was chained to the rocks and devoured by a sea monster.

As with so many star patterns, you need a vivid imagination to see her form. The brightest star in Andromeda, Alpheratz, was awarded to the constellation as recently as 1928, having previously been shared with a neighboring constellation, forming one corner of the Great Square of Pegasus.

Andromeda's greatest claim is as the home of our nearest spiral galaxy. Messier 31, sometimes wrongly termed the Andromeda Nebula, is a spiral of around a trillion stars, 2.5 million light-years away. The spiral is turned at an angle to us and is even visible to the naked eye in dark skies as an elongated blur. Binoculars will show it as a bright misty patch and amateur telescopes will pick out two of its smaller satellite galaxies: M32 and M110. A planetary nebula for small telescopes is NGC 7662.

The star Almech (Gamma Andromedae) shows as a beautiful double star in small telescopes, with contrasting orange and blue colors. Larger instruments will reveal a third companion.

AQUARIUS

APUS

The Bird of Paradise, a constellation identified in the 16th century, never flies high enough to rise above the horizon for most of the northern hemisphere. It offers little to see other than the double star Delta, a pair of 5th magnitude orange objects.

ARA

The constellation of the Altar is a compact southern grouping of faint stars. It contains NGC 6397, which is thought to be the closest globular cluster to the solar system, although it still lies 8,400 light-years away and, at magnitude 7.5, requires binoculars to be seen. NGC 6193 is an open cluster of stars for binoculars.

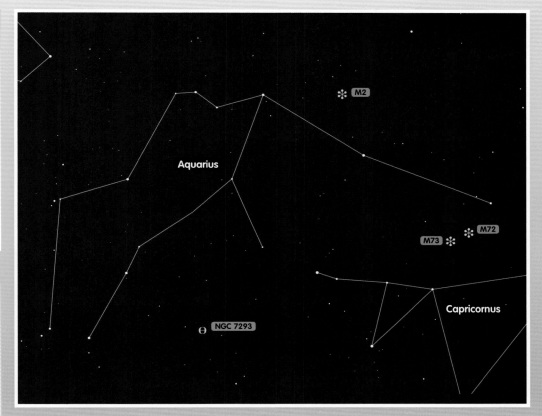

A classic constellation of the Zodiac, depicting the Water Carrier. The Sun passes through every February.

Several summer meteor showers appear to radiate from this area, notably the Eta and Delta Aquarids.

Aquarius is also where you will find the Helix Nebula or NGC 7293, the closest planetary nebula to Earth. Actually a shell of gas thrown off a star 700 light years away, the Helix is best seen in binoculars from southern latitudes, where it is higher in the sky. Space telescopes including Hubble have taken spectacular images which show it resembling a giant eye in the sky.

M2 is a globular cluster that may just be glimpsed with the naked eye. A fainter globular is M72, while M73 is simply a chance grouping of faint stars.

AQUILA

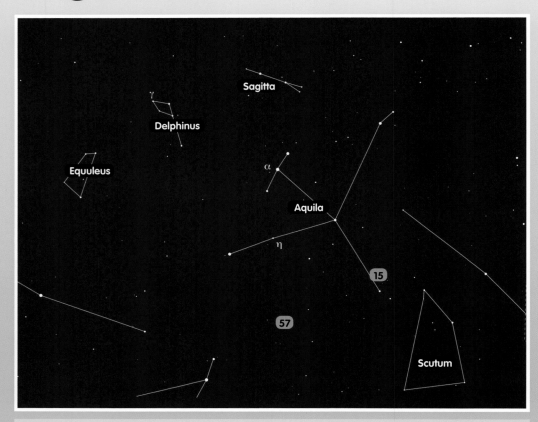

Another of several birds in the heavens, the Eagle is found easily thanks to the two attendant stars which sit either side of its brightest star, Altair. Altair also forms one point in another celestial pattern that, while not a proper constellation, is a well-known landmark in the sky: the Summer Triangle. The two other bright stars making up this feature are Deneb in Cygnus and Vega in Lyra.

Eta Aquilae is an interesting variable star of the Cepheid variety. Its brightness changes between magnitudes 3.5 and 4.3 in 7.177 days. Telescopic double stars include 15 Aquilae and 57 Aquilae.

ARIES

The Ram shows as little more than a squashed triangle (as shown on the map on p124). One of these three stars, Gamma Arietis, was among the earliest double stars spotted in the sky, although you need a telescope to be aware of this. Lambda and Pi are two other pairs. The so-called "First Point of Aries", which is where the Sun appears to cross the Celestial Equator on its journey along the ecliptic, actually now lies in the neighboring constellation of Pisces and has done so since 27BC.

CAELUM

Created by Lacaille in the mid-18th century, the Sculptor's Chisel is a small, insignificant collection of faint stars in the southern sky. Gamma is a 5th and 8th magnitude double.

AURIGA

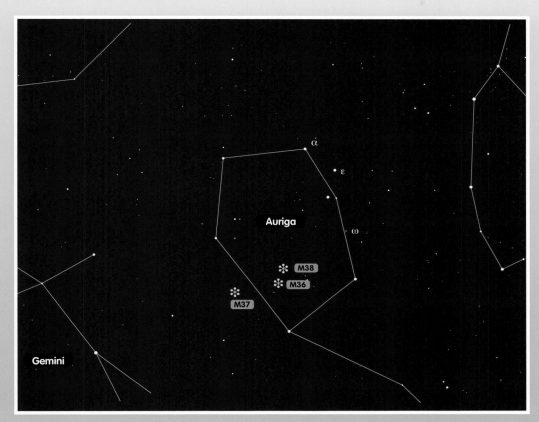

CAMELOPARDALIS

The far northern constellation of the Giraffe, stretches almost to the north celestial pole. It is largely unremarkable, however, there is a double star, Struve 1694, for small telescopes, with magnitudes of 5 and 6. Binoculars will show the cluster NGC 1502 and, with luck, the 9th magnitude spiral galaxy NGC 2403.

COLUMBA

Yet another celestial bird is the Dove. This is an obscure grouping.

The Charioteer is like a large polygon, especially if you include a star that it once shared with its neighbor, Taurus, but which has now been determined to be Beta Tauri. Its brightest star, Capella, or Alpha Aurigae, is one of the most prominent in the sky. Close by, you will find a little triangle of stars dubbed the Kids.

Auriga, is rich in star clusters and repays a sweep with binoculars. M36, M37 and M38 are all open clusters, with M37 the richest. Epsilon Aurigae is a particularly unusual star. Usually shining at magnitude 3, it undergoes a significant and regular fade every 27 years. The fades are thought to be due to an invisible companion, possibly a cloud of debris, orbiting and eclipsing the bright star. Each eclipse lasts around two years and the next is expected to begin in 2009. Omega is a double for telescopes. Its stars are 5th and 8th magnitudes.

BOÖTES

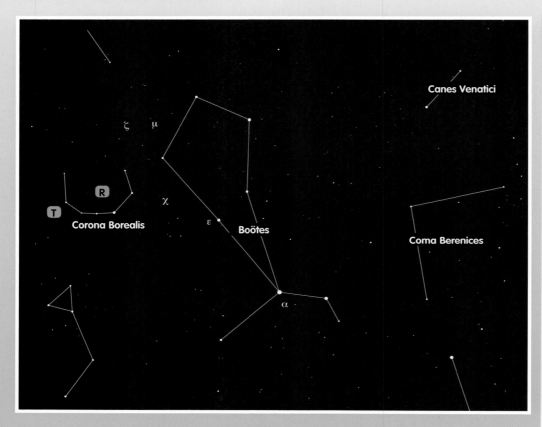

CANES VENATICI

More easily known by its English name, the Hunting Dogs, this is a minor constellation that sits beneath the tail of the Great Bear (or handle of the Plough, if you see it as such).

Unremarkable in itself, the star pattern contains a number of interesting deep sky objects. Most notably is M51, the Whirlpool, which is one of the finest spiral galaxies in the sky. It played a vital role in our understanding of the universe when, in 1845, Lord Rosse first detected its spiral structure using his giant telescope – then the biggest in the world – at Birr Castle, Ireland.

M3 is a 6th magnitude globular cluster. M63, M94 and M106 are other spiral galaxies that may be glimpsed with binoculars.

Another celestial character is the Herdsman, sometimes called the Bear Driver because he stands close to the Great Bear, Ursa Major, in the heavens. Arcturus, or alpha Boötes, is another of the brightest stars in the sky. It can found easily, when it's above the horizon, by following the curve of the Great Bear's tail. The star Epsilon Boötes is seen to be a double star through a telescope, with the companions having contrasting orange and blue colors. No wonder its Latin nickname is Pulcherrima, meaning "most beautiful". Other doubles include Mu at magnitudes 4 and 7 and Xi at 5 and 7.

CIRCINUS

The Compasses is another compact southern constellation created by Lacaille. It holds very little interest.

CANCER

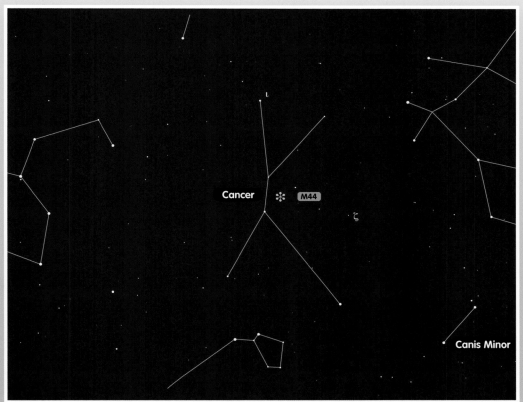

The Crab is another celestial creature within the Zodiac. It forms a spidery shape of faint stars inside which a large blur is visible to the unaided eye on a clear dark night. Binoculars reveal this to be a cloud of stars, M44, which has been given the name of Praesepe, or the Beehive Cluster.

Galileo was first to see the individual stars, managing to count 36 using his telescope. Two double stars for small telescopes are Zeta and Iota.

CANIS MINOR

Not far from its big brother sits the Little Dog. It is notable only for being home to one of the brighter stars, Procyon. This star also helps make up an unofficial grouping in the sky, the Big G. It is formed by linking Capella, in Auriga, to Castor and Pollux in Gemini, then Procyon, Sirius in Canis Major, Rigel in Orion, Aldebaran in Taurus and back into Orion to meet Betelgeuse.

CHAMAELEON

The Chameleon is a small pattern close to the south celestial pole, invented in the late 16th century.

There are few special treats, but Delta is a pair of stars that are not really connected but lie in the same direction, and NGC 3195 is a planetary nebula.

CANIS MAJOR

COMA BERENICES

Berenice's Hair contains a scattering of faint stars that appear as a "V" formation in binoculars. The constellation holds a lot of galaxies for amateur telescopes, part of the same cluster of galaxies that lies in the neighboring constellation of Virgo.

There are no fewer than eight members of Messier's famous catalog of deep sky objects in this tiny part of the sky. M53 is an 8th mag globular cluster for telescopes; M64 is a spiral known as the Black Eye galaxy because of the dark band of dust that crosses its center; other galaxies are M85, M88, M91, M98, M99 and M100.

A beautiful double star in the telescope is 24 Coma Berenicis, a 5th magnitude orange star with a 7th magnitude blue companion.

We are back to canines with the Big Dog, which sits faithfully at the feet of Orion the Hunter.

The constellation is recognized easily thanks to a number of bright stars, none more brilliant than Sirius (also known as Alpha), the brightest star in the sky. Sirius, also known as the Dog Star, appears bright largely because it lies so close to us, at a distance of just 8.6 light years, but in reality it is also burning 36 times brighter than the Sun.

M41 is an open cluster of stars that can be seen with the naked eye but looks superb in binoculars. Another is NGC 2362.

CAPRICORNUS

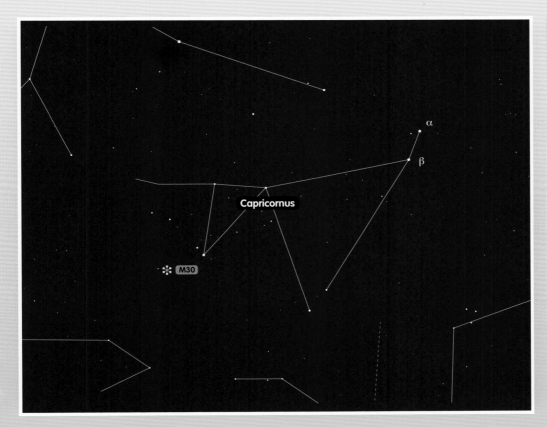

Another weird and wonderful animal is the sea goat, the smallest constellation of the Zodiac. Its pattern of stars, which more resembles a deep bowl or a laughing mouth. Its brightest star, Alpha Capricornus, is a double star that can be split with the naked eye alone. Third magnitude Beta has a 6th magnitude companion. Binoculars will show M30, an 8th magnitude globular cluster.

CORONA AUSTRALIS

The southern crown is a small and slightly less distinct replica of a similar crown in the northern sky (as shown on the map on p125). Gamma Coronae Australis is an attractive pair of 5th magnitude stars. A small instrument will show the globular cluster NGC 6541. Gamma, Kappa and Lambda are telescopic double stars.

CORONA BOREALIS

The northern crown is a compact and easily recognized circlet of stars with its brightest star set like a diadem (as shown on the map on p106). It is remarkable for having two variable stars which behave in exactly opposite ways. Amateurs keep an eye on R CrB, a 6th magnitude star visible in binoculars, because it suddenly dims at random intervals to as faint as 15th magnitude, when it is only visible in big telescopes. It is thought that this may be due to the star throwing off great clouds of soot that mask its light before they are blown away. T CrB is a faint 10th magnitude star that occasionally flares like a nova. It was first spotted at 2nd magnitude in 1866 and brightened again to 3rd magnitude in 1946. Keep an eye on Corona Borealis and you could be first to spot the next fade or flare by one of these stars. Fifth and 6th magnitude stars form the double Zeta.

CARINA

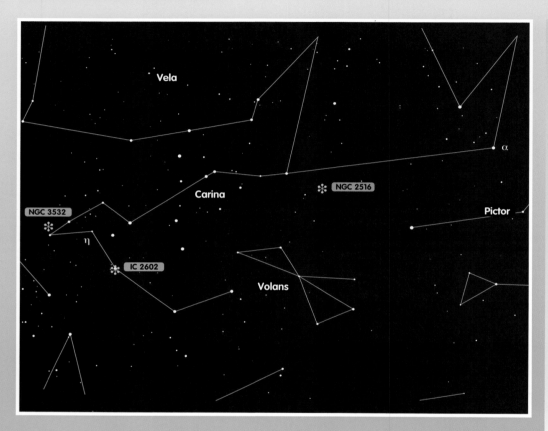

CRUX

The Southern Cross is another small patch of sky, but this time one of great interest to observers (as shown on the map on p112). It is also one of the best-known constellations, featuring on the flags of a number of countries in the southern hemisphere, including Australia and New Zealand. It lies so far south that it cannot be seen from most of the northern hemisphere. Gamma and Alpha Crucis act as pointers to the South Celestial Pole, although there is no bright star to mark its actual location. Alpha is a fine double star through a small telescope, and both stars are bright. Crux lies in the Milky Way, but close to Beta appears a large dark patch known as the Coal Sack. This is an invisible nebula that only makes its presence known to us by hiding the richness of stars that lie beyond it. Another prize that Crux holds is possibly the most beautiful star cluster in the sky, NGC 4755, or the Jewel Box.

The name means the Keel because Carina used to be part of a vast and unwieldy constellation called Argo Navis, the ship sailed by Jason and the Argonauts in Greek legend. It is a grouping for the southern hemisphere. Its brightest star, Canopus or Alpha Carinae, appears as the second most brilliant in our skies, with only Sirius being brighter. Strangely,

Carina is also home to Eta Carinae, a nova-like star embedded in a naked eye nebula. On occasions, it becomes thousands of times brighter than its usual 4th magnitude. In 1843 it briefly toppled Canopus from the No 2 spot. The Hubble Space Telescope revealed a bow tie-shaped cloud of debris ejected from Eta. A bright open cluster of stars

is IC 2602. Others visible in binoculars are NGC 2516 and NGC 3532.

CASSIOPEIA

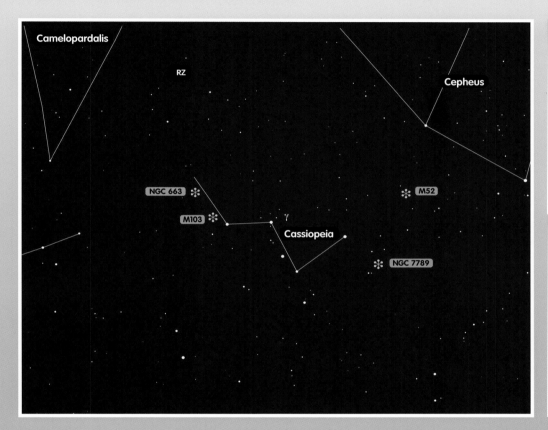

CORVUS

One more bird in the celestial aviary is the Crow, which is a tight and conspicuous pattern. A small telescope will reveal that 3rd-magnitude star Delta has a faint, 8th magnitude companion.

CRATER

This Crater represents the Cup in the heavens. There is little reason to go to this constellation as there is very little to see.

The Queen in the Chair is one of the most easily recognizable star patterns in the northern sky, resembling a "W" or "M", depending on which way up it is when you view it. A compact group, that is a circumpolar constellation for much of the northern hemisphere, meaning it never sinks below the horizon.

Conversely, it never rises from parts of the globe south of a -44 degree latitude. Cassiopeia lies more or less on the opposite side of the Pole Star to Ursa Major, so one will be high in the sky when the other is low over the horizon. It is a delightful part of the sky to sweep over with binoculars, being rich with stars of the Milky Way.

M52 and M103 are two 7th magnitude open clusters of stars. Other pretty collections, which Messier seems to have missed, are NGC 663 and NGC 7789. The star at the center, Gamma Cassiopeiae, is a peculiar variable star prone to eruptions. It has been brightening slowly and erratically over recent decades to magnitude 2.2. Keep an eye on

it: it's thought it could suddenly flare in brightness at any time. In 1572, a supernova also flared in Cassiopeia, becoming for a few months as bright as Venus. RZ Cassiopeiae is an eclipsing binary that fades from 6.4 to 7.8.

CENTAURUS

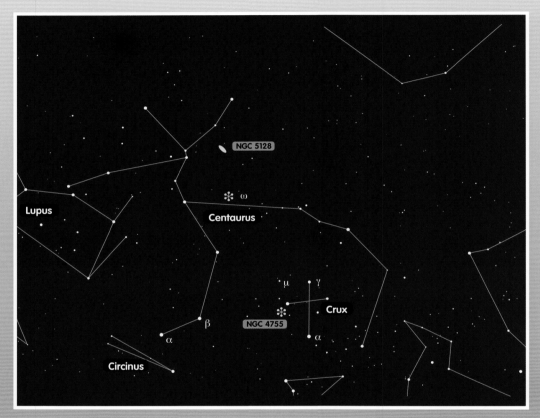

DELPHINUS

The Dolphin of the Sky is a very compact and recognizable group that looks a bit like a kite (as shown on the map on p104). It hit the astronomical headlines in 1967 when one of the most interesting novae, or exploding stars, of the 20th century flared there. There is little today of particular interest, however, although Gamma is a double star with 4th and 5th magnitude components which may be split in small telescopes.

EQUULEUS

The Baby Horse, or Foal, is also one of the smallest constellations (as shown on the map on p104). Gamma, an easy double star for binocular observers, has companions of magnitudes 4.5 and 6.

Half man, half horse, the Centaur rides deep in the southern sky. It sprawls over a large area and, includes two bright stars close together: Alpha and Beta Centauri. Alpha's claim to fame is that it is the closest star to the Sun, which helps explain why it is the third brightest star in the night sky. It is really a triple star system. Small instruments will show Alpha as two bright stars, but there is also a faint orbiting companion, Proxima Centauri, which is the nearest to us in the group. Centaurus is also where you will find the finest globular cluster in the entire sky. Despite the single star's label of Omega Centauri, it is a cloud of millions of closely-packed stars. A bright blur seen with the naked eye by southern observers, covering a larger area of the sky than the Full Moon, but binoculars and telescopes will show its full glory. Some astronomers believe Omega to be the remains of a dwarf galaxy that was absorbed by our own Milky Way. A fuzzy 7th magnitude patch visible in binoculars is a powerful broadcaster for radio telescopes. Centaurus A, also known as NGC 5128, is thought to be two colliding galaxies.

CEPHEUS

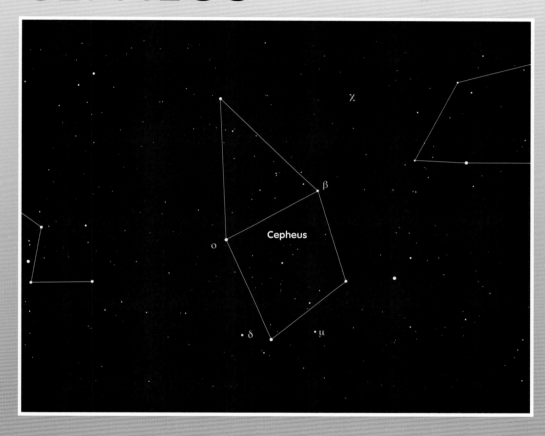

DORADO

The Swordfish is a southern constellation created in the 16th century. It is interesting as it contains a bright comp-anion galaxy to the Milky Way within its borders. The Large Magellanic Cloud can be clearly seen as a bright blur in dark skies but lies around 180,000 light years away. Within the LMC is a remarkable nebula called the Tarantula, because it resembles a spider in photos. It looks like a fuzzy star to the naked eye. The closest supernova in recent times was spotted in the LMC in 1987. Beta is a bright Cepheid variable.

In legend, the King of Ethiopia was Cassiopeia's spouse. This constellation, bordering Cassiopeia and close to the north celestial pole, is inconspicuous because its stars are not particularly bright. However, it's not difficult to make out a house shape, and it contains some interesting stars. Perhaps the most important is Delta Cephei, which gave its name to a special type of variable star which helped give us a sense of scale in the universe. These Cepheids vary in a very regular way, and it was discovered that the time it takes one to complete one cycle or variation is directly related to its luminosity. By comparing the apparent magnitude to the real brightness, it was therefore possible to determine how far away they are. Delta Cephei's brightness varies between 3.4 and 4.3 magnitude in 5.366 days. Another naked eye variable star in Cepheus is Mu Cephei, nicknamed the Garnet Star because it is one of the reddest stars known. Binoculars will bring out this red giant's color and will help to monitor the irregular pattern of changes in brightness, ranging from 3.6 to 5.1 magnitude. U Cephei is an eclipsing variable fading from 6.6 to 9.3. Interesting double stars are Beta, Delta, Xi and Omicron.

CETUS

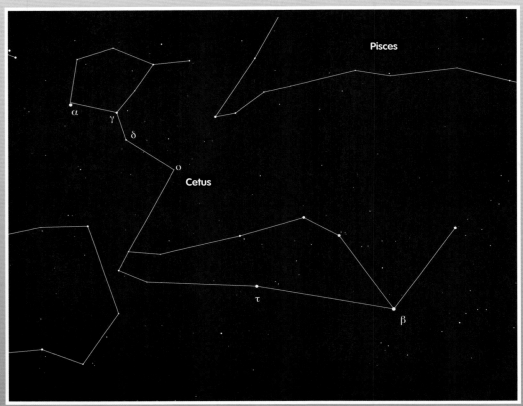

DRACO

We are back in the northern hemisphere for this snake-like pattern named the Dragon. The four stars that form the beast's head are not difficult to find, but it is out of reach for much of the southern hemisphere.

Nu Draconis is a splendid double star in binoculars, both stars being white and of 5th magnitude. Other interesting multiple-star targets are the doubles Omicron and Psi, plus the triple systems 16-17 and 40-41.

It's not impossible to see the shape of a whale in the Sea Monster, although traditionally its head was supposed to be the tail and vice versa. The bright star Beta makes a very fine whale's snout and a little close pattern of stars below Aries form a realistic tail. Three of these stars – Alpha, Gamma and Delta – also form a pattern very like

Aries, so be careful you don't mistake them. Cetus contains two stars of particular interest. The first is Omicron Ceti, which has the nickname Mira, meaning "the wonderful", as it undergoes an extreme change in brightness every year. Usually its range is from 3rd or 4th magnitude at its brightest, to between 8th and 10th at its faintest, in a period

of 331 days. But sometimes it becomes really bright, as in March 2007 when it reached 2.2 magnitude. The second, Tau Ceti is a star only moderately bright in the whale's belly. But it is interesting because it is similar to our Sun, if slightly smaller, and lies just 11.68 light years away from us. To the disappointment of professional

astronomers, no planets have yet been detected, although we know it is surrounded by a disk of dust and debris. Alpha and Gamma Ceti are double stars.

CYGNUS

The Swan is often known as the Northern Cross. It is far bigger than its southern rival and for once it's not difficult to imagine this as a bird in flight with a long neck and outstretched wings. It lies in the Milky Way and, as a result, contains a lot within its boundaries that will appeal to the astronomer. Cygnus's brightest star, Alpha Cygni (also known as Deneb) is one of the galaxy's most luminous stars. It is one of the three bright stars which make up the unofficial pattern of the Summer Triangle. At the other end of the longer bar of the cross is Beta Cygni, otherwise known as Albireo. This is one of the most beautiful double stars in the sky, with a bright 3rd magnitude yellow star joined by a 5th magnitude blue companion. The contrasting colors are splendid to see, even in binoculars. Fourth magnitude Omicron has a 5th magnitude companion. One of Cygnus's fainter naked eye stars, 61 Cygni, is another binary system and is interesting because it is one of the closest stars to our own

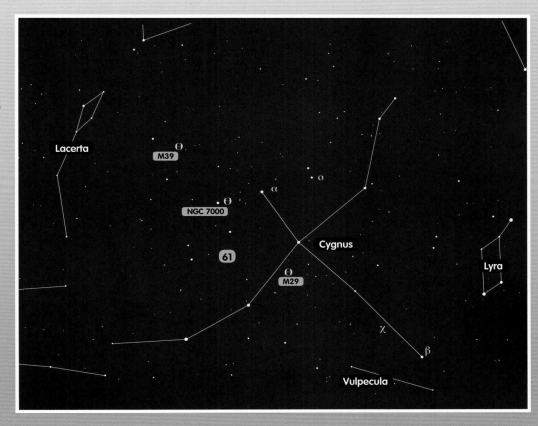

Sun, lying just 11 light years away. It has the distinction of being the first star to have its distance measured by parallax. This technique involves observing a close star's position against distant background stars from points on opposite sides of the Earth's orbit, a long enough baseline to reveal a tiny but detectable difference. It is

believed that 61 Cygni might be a star that has planets. Chi Cygni is a long period variable star, like Mira. It can reach 4th magnitude at brightest but becomes as faint as 12th magnitude with a period of 407 days. Professional astronomers are interested in an intense source of X-rays called Cygnus X-1. This is thought to be a black hole, the first to be

identified. Binoculars will reveal a bright patch close to Deneb that has been dubbed North America Nebula, because its shape vaguely resembles that continent. In truly clear and dark conditions, it may be seen with the naked eye.

GEMINI

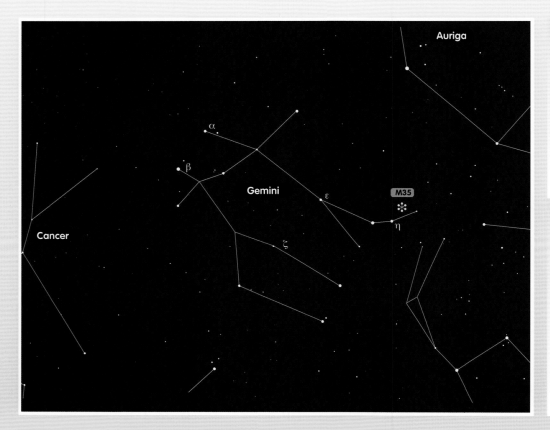

FORNAX

There is little to see in this constellation of the southern sky. The brightest star, Alpha, can only manage 4th magnitude but those with a decent telescope may appreciate its 6th magnitude partner.

GRUS

The Crane is yet another bird let loose in the heavens, but its flight is one for southern observers. There are two double stars visible with the naked eye. Delta Gruis is a pair of 4th magnitude stars and Mu has two stars of 5th magnitude.

The Twins are part of the Zodiac and, with two strikingly bright stars called Castor (also known as Alpha) and Pollux (also known as Beta), offer a variety of interesting objects to observe. The two main stars also form part of the Big G described earlier. A small telescope will show magnitude 1.6 Castor as a close pair of bright stars of 2nd and 3rd magnitude. There are actually six stars in Castor's system. Eta Geminorum is a particularly interesting bright variable. Usually its brightness ranges from around 3.1 to 3.5, but the star is also eclipsed by an invisible companion just over every eight years, so that it can dim to around magnitude 3.9. Another variable star is Zeta Gem, which varies by only four tenths of a magnitude in 10.2 days. A fine sight in binoculars is the fuzzy patch that is the star cluster M35. A telescope will reveal the stars within it. Gemini is also the source of the radiant of one of the year's strongest meteor showers.

The Geminids might be better known if they did not occur in midwinter for northern latitudes. A night's viewing could be rewarded by the sight of several bright meteors in a matter of minutes.

HERCULES

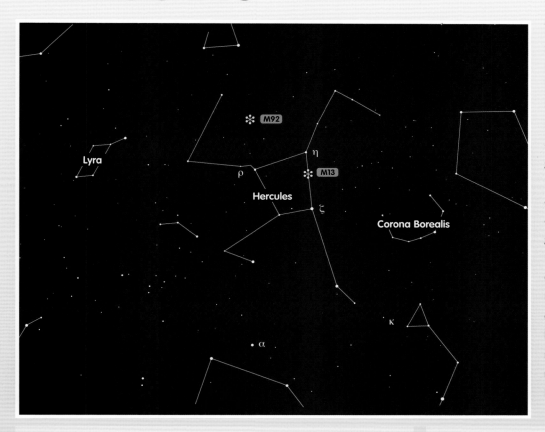

The hero of Greek legend stands proud with his club held high in this prominent northern constellation. Hercules's torso is drawn fairly clearly by four stars. Between the two at top right, Eta and Theta, can be found a bright blur that is M13, the finest globular cluster in the northern sky. It contains around 300,000 stars and is easy to pick out in binoculars and any telescope. M92 is another globular cluster for binoculars in Hercules, that is rather unfairly overlooked because of its brighter rival. Alpha Herculis is a naked eye variable star. This red giant's brightness ranges between magnitudes 3 and 4 in a fairly unpredictable fashion. Double stars include Rho, Kappa and 95 Herculis.

HYDRA

The Water Snake is an inconspicuous constellation that is also the largest in the sky. Only its brightest star, Alphard, is brighter than magnitude 3. The constellation contains three Messier objects: M48 is a cluster of around 80 stars that can be seen in binoculars; M68 is a small globular cluster of 8th magnitude; and M83 is a fine spiral galaxy viewed in all its glory from above. Look, too, for the planetary nebula NGC 3242. Small telescopes will show the double stars 27 Hydrae, 54 Hydrae and I Hydrae.

HOROLOGIUM

The Pendulum Clock is a relatively modern constellation created in the southern sky by Lacaille in the 18th century. Binocular users may watch the red semi-regular variable TW Horologii change its brightness between magnitudes 5 and 6. A telescope will be needed to follow R Horologii through its 400-day cycle.

LEO

HYDRUS

There is a second southern Water Snake in the heavens. The only target within it of minor interest is the double star Pi Hydrae, two 5th magnitude stars that may be viewed with binoculars or even the naked eye.

INDUS

This constellation was created in the late 16th century to represent the American Indian. There is little to observe save for the double star Theta Indi, which may be split by small telescopes into 5th and 7th magnitude companions.

LEO MINOR

The Lion Cub sits above its mighty adult relative, . Unfortunately, there is nothing of interest to view within this small grouping.

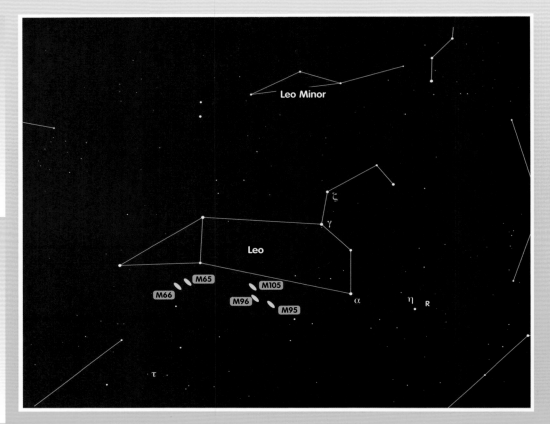

This is a constellation that resembles the lion it represents. A backward question mark represents the head and a triangle of stars the haunches of the king of the jungle. Leo is part of the Zodiac through which the Sun travels.There are several galaxies including the spirals M65 and M66 for small telescopes. Fainter spirals are M95 and M96. M105 is a faint elliptical galaxy that is challenging to find. An interesting variable star is R Leonis, which fades from 5th to 10th magnitude with a period of around 310 days.

Double star observers may enjoy spotting Gamma, which shows 2nd and 3rd magnitude companions in a telescope. Zeta is revealed to be three unrelated stars in the same line of sight when checked out with binoculars. Orange star Tau Leonis is visible in binoculars, showing a 5th magnitude star with a 7th magnitude companion. Leo is also home of the Leonid meteor shower which has produced some spectacular storms in the past.

LYRA

The Lyre, an ancient form of the harp, is a striking little pattern that is easy to locate. A major reason is that its main star, Vega (Alpha), is one of the brightest in the sky. It is the brightest, too, of the three stars that make up the Summer Triangle, together with Deneb in Cygnus and Altair in Aquila. Delta is a double star. A magnitude 6 blue star is accompanied by a red giant star that fluctuates between magnitudes 4 and 5.

Epsilon is the best-known multiple star system in the heavens. The keen-sighted will spot two 5th magnitude stars close together, but a telescope will reveal each to be formed of two stars.

Look at Zeta in binoculars to find another double, this time with components of magnitudes 4 and 6. Beta Lyrae is the best-known member of a class of variable star, the bright eclipsing variables. Both components of this system are bright and they orbit each other so closely that they are egg-shaped and almost touching. This results

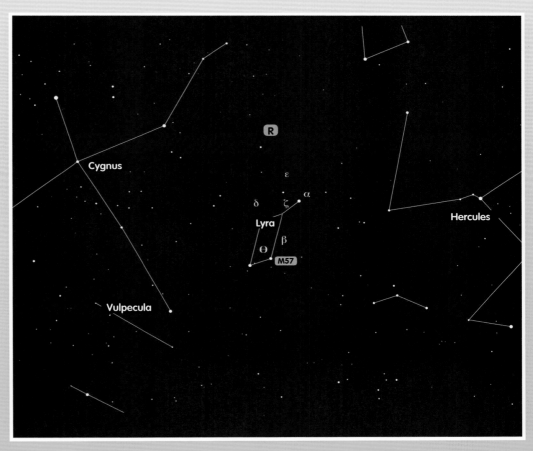

in a constant brightness exchange as the stars dance around each other, varying between magnitude 3.4 and 4.3 in a little under 13 days. You won't be able to see these two stars individually, but a small telescope will reveal another 8th magnitude blue companion plus two other 9th magnitude stars

close by. R Lyrae is a semi-regular variable that fluctuates between 3.9 and 5.

There is a further challenge in Lyra – the famous Ring Nebula, M57. This is easy enough to locate, midway between the lower two stars in Lyra's diamond, but you need transparent skies and a powerful

telescope to make out very much. The radiant of the Lyrids, a meteor show active in April, lies in this constellation.

ERIDANUS

Fittingly for a constellation named the River, this star grouping meanders a long way across the sky from its "source" Alpha, a bright star that lies too far south to be seen from many northern countries.

The other end of this cosmic waterway is right up alongside the stars of Orion and visible throughout the world.

Epsilon Eridani, clearly visible at magnitude 3.7, is another star of great interest to those hunting for planets, as it lies only 10.7 light years away and is of a similar type to the Sun. Star Trek fans will recognize it as Mr Spock's home star, around which Vulcan supposedly revolved. Small telescopes will split the double stars Theta and 32 Eridani. Also look for the 9th magnitude planetary nebula NGC 1535.

LEPUS

The Hare is found directly beneath the feet of Orion the Hunter. It is not striking but there are treasures to be found. Gamma Leporis is an easy binocular double star with a yellow 4th magnitude star and an orange 6th magnitude companion.

Another interesting star is the variable R Leporis, a deeply red star that fades from 6th to 10th magnitude with a cycle of 430 days. It is nicknamed Hind's Crimson star after a 19th century observer who noted its intense hue.

Small telescopes will reveal M79, an 8th magnitude globular cluster. Nearby is a group of five stars in one system that form the cluster NGC 2017.

LIBRA

The Scales are a constellation of the Zodiac. Alpha, a 3rd magnitude star with a 5th magnitude companion, rejoices in the splendid name Zubenelgenubi.

Iota Librae can be seen through a telescope to have three companions. Some say Beta Librae looks decidedly green — you should check for yourself. Delta Librae is an Algol-type eclipsing binary star with a range from 4.8 to 5.9.

LACERTA

The Lizard is one of the sky's least interesting constellations. It lacks anything worth viewing for an observer with only a small telescope.

LUPUS

Another member of the celestial menagerie is the Wolf. Telescopes will be needed to tackle its horde of double stars: Epsilon Lupi (mags 3 and 9), Kappa (4 and 6), Mu (4 and 7), Xi (5 and 6) and Pi (a 5th magnitude pair).

Binoculars will show the large star cluster NGC 5822.

LYNX

The Lynx is the most inconspicuous constellation. Small telescopes will reveal that 5 Lyncis is an orange star of 5th magnitude with an 8th mag partner.

12 Lyncis is a bluish star, also of 5th magnitude, with companions of 6th and 8th magnitude.

ORION

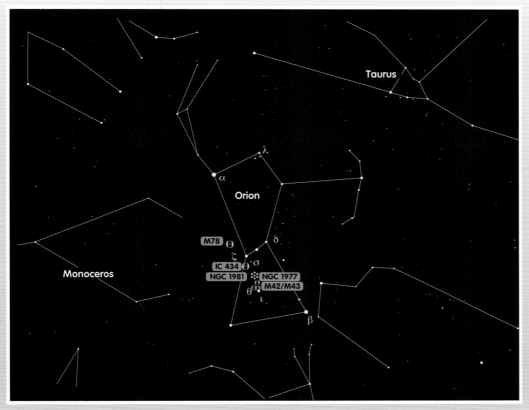

The Hunter is perhaps the best known of the constellations, and because he stands across the Celestial Equator, he can be seen from all parts of the world.

Orion contains some fascinating objects for the amateur astronomer. Alpha Orionis, or Betelgeuse, on the Hunter's left shoulder, is a red giant star, 427 light years away, that varies erratically in brightness between magnitude 0.4 and 1.3. Some believe it could be on the verge of becoming a supernova within the next 1,000 years. If it does, it will be bright enough to be seen in daylight for several months.

Beta Orionis, or Rigel, is a brilliant, blue-white star shining at magnitude 0.1 – compare its color with that of Betelgeuse. It is also a luminous supergiant nearly 48,000 times brighter than our Sun and lying 900 light years away. Double stars include Delta (mags 2 and 7), Zeta (2 and 4), Iota (3 and 7), Lambda (4 and 6) and Sigma (4 and 7). Theta is actually a wide and complex pair of stars that can be found in Orion's most famous feature – the Great Orion Nebula, a bright celestial nursery of newborn stars and one of the outstanding sights in the sky. Theta1 is a pattern of four of these infant stars that are illuminating the nebula, which was given two labels by Messier, M42 and M43, for its two brighter regions. Fainter stars may be seen in larger telescopes. More wisps of nebulosity, labeled NGC 1977, can be seen just to the north in small telescopes. Another nebula, IC 434, close to Zeta Orionis, is famed for a dark silhouette that resembles a chess piece. However, the Horsehead Nebula is virtually impossible to spot in amateur telescopes. For binoculars, there is an open star cluster NGC 1981. The Orionids are a strong meteor shower visible in October that are the product of debris from Halley's Comet.

PEGASUS

The Winged Horse is mainly seen as an easily recognized Great Square rather than an animal, although the four stars of that square include one that was awarded in the last century to neighboring Andromeda.

The bright magnitude 2 star Epsilon Pegasi has a 9th magnitude star visible in small telescopes. A variable star worth watching is Beta Pegasi, which fluctuates erratically between magnitudes 2 and 3.

Binoculars or a small telescope are enough to spot the splendid 6th magnitude globular cluster M15.

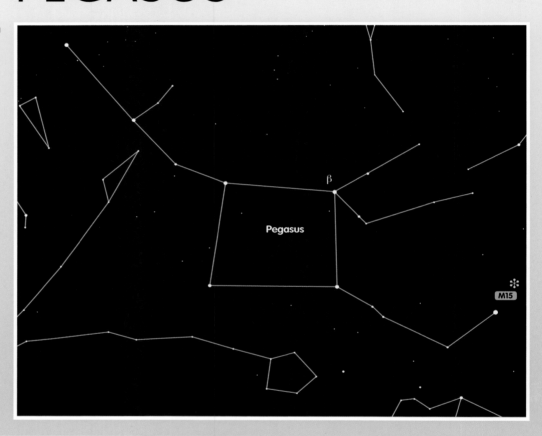

OCTANS

You can't get further south than the Octant. Invented by Lacaille, it is the constellation containing and centered on the South Celestial Pole. There is no bright Pole Star to mark it, unlike Polaris in the north, but the faint mag 5.5 star Sigma is actually closer to its pole than is its northern equivalent. The only other object of interest is Lambda Octantis, a double star with 5th magnitude yellow and 8th magnitude white companions.

OPHIUCHUS

The Serpent Bearer straddles the Celestial Equator. It is rich with deep sky gems, containing seven objects from Messier's catalog. M9, M10, M12, M14, M19, M62 and M107 are all globular clusters for binoculars or small telescopes. An open cluster for binoculars, lying close to Beta Ophiuchi, is IC 4665. The most interesting object in Ophiuchus is Barnard's Star, which a small telescope will show shining at magnitude 9.5. Lying a little under six light years from us, its motion across the sky is easily detectable over a relatively short time.

PERSEUS

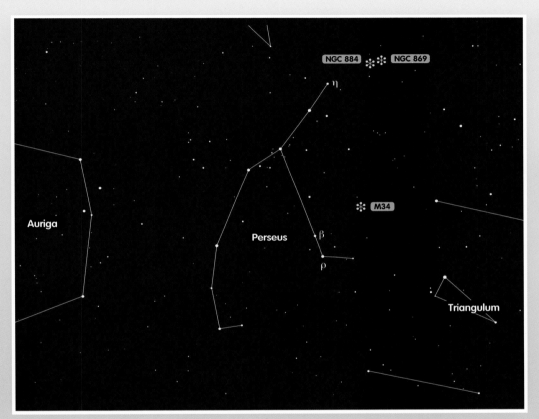

PICTOR

The Painter's Easel is, unfortunately, an empty canvas when it comes to targets for the amateur astronomer.

PHOENIX

The Phoenix is the most unusual of the birds flying the heavens, being the one that rose from the ashes.

A challenge for small telescopes is the close pair of 4th magnitude stars Beta Phoenicis. Another double, Zeta, is a 4th magnitude eclipsing binary with an 8th magnitude companion.

The Greek hero of legend is another of the sky's characters. It lies in the Milky Way and is a constellation with many interesting objects. Check out Eta Persei, with a small telescope, to discern an orange 4th magnitude star with a blue 9th magnitude companion. There are two interesting variable stars in Perseus, both visible with the naked eye and coincidentally lying close together. Beta Persei is Algol, the prototype of the dark eclipsing variables. These are twin stars, one small and bright, one large and dim, close together and orbiting in our line of sight. When the dark star passes in front of the bright one, the light from the combined pair fades from 2.2 to 3.5. The eclipses happen every two days, 21 hours.

Rho Persei is a totally different type, a red giant, semi-regular variable, with a range from magnitude 3.3 to 4. The jewels in Perseus's crown are its famous Double Cluster, NGC 869 and NGC 884. Binoculars are enough to show these rich concentrations of stars, but in small telescopes they sparkle like diamonds.

Another bright cluster is M34. The Perseid meteor shower in August is one of the strongest for northern hemisphere observers, with a rate of 100 an hour under ideal conditions.

PISCES

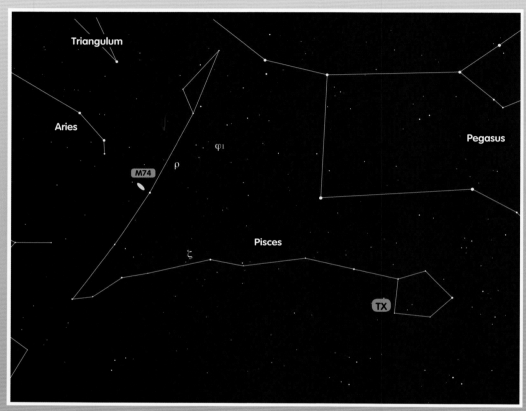

PISCIS AUSTRINUS

Another fish swims among the southern stars. Though hardly prominent, it does have one very bright star, 1st magnitude Fomalhaut. Small telescopes will separate the 4th magnitude star Beta from an 8th magnitude star close by.

PUPPIS

This represents the stern of the former huge constellation of Argo Navis. It lies in the Milky Way and its attractive offerings include the double stars Xi Puppis, a 3rd magnitude yellow star with an orange 5th magnitude companion, and k Puppis, twin 4th magnitude stars.

Two variable stars are L2 Puppis, a red giant varying between magnitudes 3 and 6, and V Puppis, an eclipsing binary ranging between magnitudes 4.5 and 5.1. Fine star clusters for binoculars are M47 and NGC 2451.

A forked pattern represents the two Fishes, an inconspicuous but important constellation in the Zodiac because it contains the point where the Ecliptic crosses the Celestial Equator. This is the point where the Sun passes at the time of the vernal equinox in March.

Easy double stars in small telescopes are Zeta Piscium (magnitudes 5 and 6), Rho (both 5th magnitude) and Psi1 (both 5th magnitude). A bright binocular variable is TX Piscium, a red giant that varies from 5th to 6th magnitude. M74, an unimpressive faint blur in small telescopes, shows itself as a fine spiral galaxy in professional photographs.

SCULPTOR

The Sculptor is in the southern sky . An interesting star for binocular users is the red giant R Sculptoris, with a range from magnitude 5.8 to 7.7. There are two galaxies for small telescopes: the edge-on spiral NGC 55 and NGC 253.

SAGITTARIUS

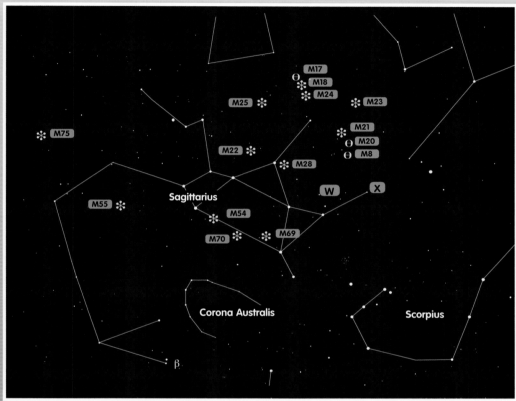

PYXIS

A further part of the defunct Argo Navis, that offers little of interest for amateur astronomers.

At rare intervals, a 14th magnitude star, T Pyxidis, flares like a nova to around 6th magnitude.

RETICULUM

The Net is another tiny and obscure southern constellation. Binoculars will clearly show Zeta Reticuli, a pair of yellow, 5th magnitude stars.

The Zodiacal constellation of the Archer actually looks like a teapot. It's a treasure trove of interesting objects for observers.

For double star observers, there is Beta Sagitarii, two stars that can be split by the naked eye. The more northerly star has a 7th magnitude partner. Two Cepheid variables are W Sagittarii, with a magnitude range from 4.3 and 5, plus X Sagittarii, fluctuating between magnitude 4.3 and 4.9.

There are no less than 15 Messier deep sky objects in Sagittarius. M8 is the Lagoon Nebula, a large, naked eye gas cloud shining at 5th magnitude. It contains a cluster of stars, NGC 6530, that can be viewed in binoculars.

Another blur for binoculars is the nebula M17. M18 is an 8th magnitude open cluster. M20 is the Trifid Nebula, a gas cloud with dark, dusty patterns that can only be made out with large amateur telescopes. M21 is a star cluster that lies in the same region. M22, M28, M54, M55, M69, M70 and M75 are globular clusters of magnitude 6.5, 8.5, 8.5, 7, 9, 9 and 9.5. M23 and M25 are bright open clusters while M24 is a dense cloud of stars in the Milky Way.

SCORPIUS

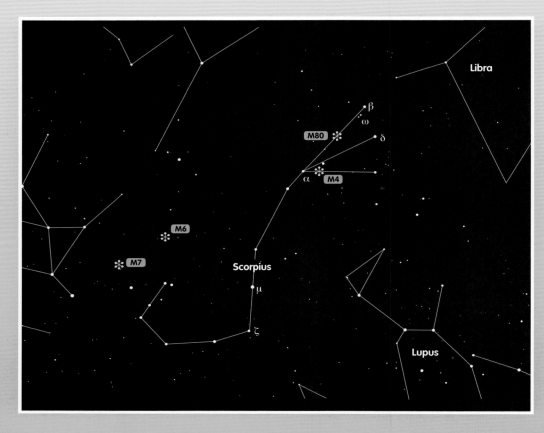

SCUTUM

The Shield is a tiny but rewarding constellation close to the Celestial Equator. The Milky Way passes through it, presenting some fine sweeping for binoculars. R Scuti is a yellow giant variable star that may be followed in brightness between 5th and 8th magnitudes.

M11 is a splendid scattering of stars for small telescopes and even binoculars, with the nickname the Wild Duck Cluster. M26 is a less spectacular open cluster.

Also in the Zodiac is the Scorpion. The curve of its stars make it closely resemble the creature that it represents, right down to the sting in the tail. Its brightest star, Antares (Alpha), has a name that translates as "the Rival of Mars", because its red color compares with that planet when it passes through the area. With a large enough telescope, you might spot

Antares' blue 6th magnitude companion. Scorpius is another Zodiacal treasure chest, although its position favors more southerly observers. Beta Scorpii is a good double star target for small telescopes, with 3rd and 5th magnitude companions. Zeta is a 4th and 5th magnitude pair that can be split with the naked eye, but the stars are not really related. Also unrelated are the

two stars marking Omega. Mu shows two bluish stars of 3rd and 4th magnitude.

Turn a small telescope on Xi to find a system of four stars, of magnitudes 4, 7, 7 and 8. Keep an eye on Delta up near the Scorpion's head, because it unexpectedly brightened by around half a magtnitude in recent years. This is thought to

be due to eruptions of gas from the star.

There are four objects from Messier's catalog: M4 and M80 are globular clusters for binoculars or small telescopes, while M6 and M7 are fine open star clusters.

MICROSCOPIUM

The Microscope is another inconspicuous southern constellation, created in the 18th century by Lacaille. It is devoid of interest.

MUSCA

The Fly buzzes far in the southern sky and Crux is its neighbor.

Telescopes reveal that the bluish, 3rd magnitude star Beta Muscae is formed of two close 4th magnitude companions. Theta is another double with 5th and 7th magnitude components.

MENSA

The Table Mountain, a "modern" 18th century constellation, lies to the far south. There is little to see in this grouping of stars, although it does include a small part of the Large Magellanic Cloud, a satellite galaxy of our Milky Way.

MONOCEROS

The unicorn lies pinned between two heavenly dogs – Canis Major and Canis Minor – and straddles the Celestial Equator. It is not easy to spot, with attention being grabbed by its neighbors, including Gemini and Orion.

Despite its feeble appearance, there is much to see within it. Stars with partners include the fine Beta Monocerotis, a group of three bluish suns of 4th, 5th and 6th magnitude. Binoculars show that 4th-magnitude Delta appears to have a companion a magnitude fainter, but they just happen to lie closely in line.

For another genuine double, check out Epsilon, where a yellow 4th magnitude star contrasts with a blue 7th magnitude star. Binoculars will also bring into view a number of star clusters, including M50, NGC 2232, NGC 2244 and NGC 2264. The infant stars of NGC 2244 are surrounded by the remnants of their birth, the gas of the Rosette Nebula. A bright but unrelated star, 12 Monocerotis, lies in front of the cluster. One of the stars in the cluster NGC 2264 is an irregular variable star with a range between magnitudes 4 and 5.

PAVO

Another bird, the Peacock, looks a lot less dazzling than its real-life cousin in this constellation of the far south. Variable star observers can follow Kappa Pavonis, which ranges between mag 3.9 and 4.8 in just over nine days. There is also a 7th magnitude globular cluster, NGC 6752, visible in binoculars.

NORMA

The Set Square has two true double stars, Epsilon and Iota Normae, for telescopes. Each comprises a 5th magnitude star with an 8th magnitude companion. Gamma appears double and is easy to split with the naked eye, but the 4th and 5th magnitude yellow stars are really not connected.

Binoculars will show one large star cluster, NGC 6087. It is formed from more than 30 stars including a Cepheid variable, S Normae, shining at around 6th magnitude.

TAURUS

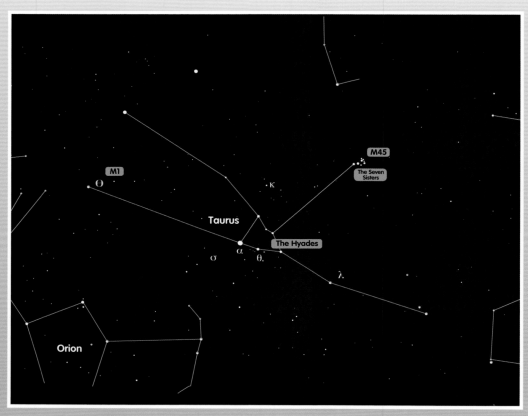

TELESCOPIUM

Disappointingly for a pattern named after the telescope, there is nothing worth viewing in this southern group created by Lacaille.

TRIANGULUM

The Triangle is a compact group between Andromeda and Aries (as shown on the map on p102). It holds one treasure, M33, nicknamed the Pinwheel Galaxy. This is a large and faint member of our local group of galaxies, which can make it a challenge to find in telescopes. However, if the sky is clear and dark, it may be seen with the naked eye.

The Bull is a prominent constellation of the Zodiac, pictured making a charge at neighbor Orion. It contains two striking star clusters, the Hyades and the Pleiades. The Hyades are spread out in a "V" shape that represents the Bull's head. The constellation's brightest star, 1st magnitude Aldebaran (Alpha), appears at one end of this "V" but is really at half the distance of the cluster which lies 150 light years away from us. Nearby M45, the Pleiades, is the most spectacular open cluster in the heavens. It was nicknamed the Seven Sisters – see how many you can count with the naked eye – but telescopes will reveal dozens more stars. Long-exposure photos show the young stars embedded in wisps of nebulosity. Double stars for binoculars include Theta (3rd and 4th magnitude) in the Hyades, Kappa (4th and 5th) and Sigma (both 5th). An interesting variable star is Lambda, an eclipsing binary with a cycle between magnitudes 3.4 and 4.1. Also in Taurus is the first object in Messier's catalog, M1, the remains of a supernova blast in 1054. It is nicknamed the Crab Nebula from the shape of its filaments of gas, but small telescopes will reveal only a tiny hazy patch.

URSA MAJOR

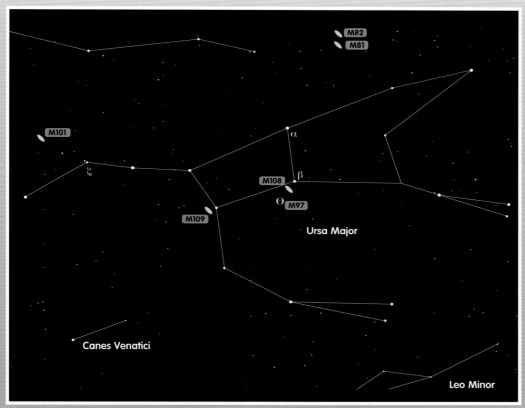

TUCANA

The Toucan would not be very interesting if it was not for the presence of a bright satellite galaxy called the Small Magellanic Cloud and 47 Tucanae, the second best globular cluster in the sky. This can be seen with the naked eye. Sadly, both are hidden from much of the northern hemisphere.

The Small Magellanic Cloud lies 200,000 light years away and contains hundreds of millions of stars. It appears as a bright patch of mist to the naked eye but is fascinating to sweep with binoculars. Beta Tucanae is a 4th and 5th magnitude double star in binoculars, but a telescope reveals that the brighter star has actually two components.

The Great Bear is one of the best-known constellations, with its seven main stars also dubbed the Plough and the Big Dipper.

Bayer generally awarded Greek letters to stars in order of brightness, but obviously found that too much trouble here and, instead, gave the first seven in the order they lined up. Alpha and Beta Ursae Majoris are also known as the Pointers, because they indicate the direction of the Pole Star. Zeta, also known as Mizar, can be seen with keen eyes to have a 4th magnitude companion, Alcor. Small telescopes will reveal a 4th magnitude star between them. Although you can't separate them, both Mizar and Alcor have been found to be close binary stars too.

There are some great galaxies for observers. M81 and M82 are a close pair in binoculars, one a spiral and one cigar-shaped. M101 is seen as a face-on spiral in photos. M108 and M109 are two fainter spirals. M97 is the Owl Nebula, a planetary nebula for telescopes. Ursa Major is also the source of the Ursids, a meteor shower visible in late December.

URSA MINOR

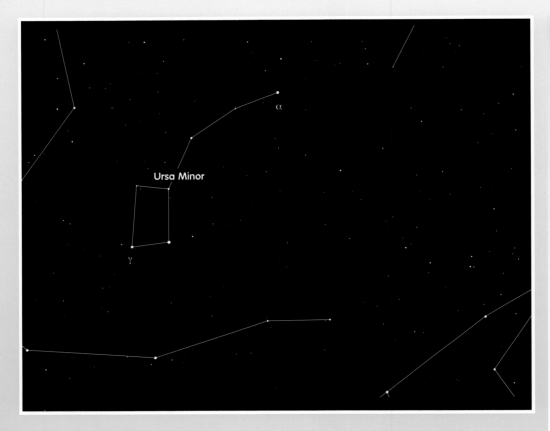

Ursa Minor

The Little Bear wraps itself around the North Celestial Pole. Second magnitude Alpha Ursae Minoris, known as Polaris or the Pole Star, actually lies a degree from the Pole. It has a 9th magnitude companion in small telescopes.

Gamma is 3rd magnitude but keen eyes will spot a 5th magnitude star close by. They are not related.

SAGITTA

The Arrow is a tiny star grouping within the Milky Way. Turn a small telescope on the 5th magnitude star Zeta Sagittae to spot a 9th magnitude companion. M71 is a 7th magnitude star cluster that may be picked out in binoculars.

TRIANGULUM AUSTRALE

The Southern Triangle. There is not a lot to spot but use binoculars to view NGC 6025, an open cluster.

SERPENS

The Serpent is the only constellation to come in two sections: a head (Serpens Caput) and tail (Serpens Cauda) on either side of Ophiuchus. They are still considered a single constellation.

Bright double stars are Delta Serpentis and Theta, each with 4th and 5th magnitude components. For star clusters, turn your binoculars on Tau Serpentis and M16, which clear skies may reveal is embedded in a cloud of gas. This is the Eagle Nebula, famous for the finger-like Pillars of Creation pictured by the Hubble. M5 is a superb globular cluster that is almost a rival for M13 in Hercules in the northern sky.

SEXTANS

The Sextant is a small and feeble 17th-century constellation. There is very little of interest here.

VIRGO

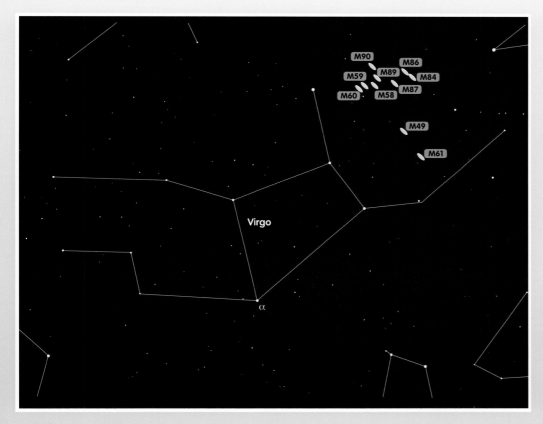

Within the image:
- M90
- M86
- M89
- M84
- M59
- M58
- M87
- M60
- M49
- M61
- Virgo
- α

VELA

The sail is the final part of the old broken-up sailing ship Argo Navis in the southern sky. Binoculars will split Gamma Velorum into a 2nd and 4th magnitude pair. Telescopes reveal two more 9th and 10th magnitude stars in the system.

The Milky Way runs through Vela and offers two binocular star clusters: IC 2391 and NGC 2547.

VULPECULA

The last of the constellations is small and faint but has some interesting inhabitants. Alpha Vulpeculae is a 4th magnitude red star. Binoculars show an unrelated 6th magnitude star close by.

A fun asterism is the Coathanger, a pattern of stars that looks just like that household item. Vulpecula is also home to M27, the Dumbbell, which is said to be the easiest planetary nebula to make out in the sky.

The virgin of the Zodiac is not a terribly prominent shape, although it has one bright, 1st magnitude star, Spica (also known as Alpha).

The Autumnal Equinox lies in Virgo, marking the point where the Ecliptic again crosses the Celestial Equator. Virgo's main prize is a huge cluster of distant galaxies around 65 million light-years away. M49, M58, M59, M60, M61, M84, M86, M87, M89 and M90 are brighter members of the cluster, which may be spotted in small telescopes. Another famous galaxy, M104, lies somewhat closer and is nicknamed the Sombrero as it resembles the hat.

VOLANS

The Flying Fish is a faint and a far southern grouping. Gamma Volantis is a 4th magnitude white star with a 6th magnitude yellow companion.

EQUIPMENT NEEDED TO BE AN ASTRONOMER

Astronomers do not need to pay out on a lot of expensive gear to get started. The truth is that you don't need any equipment to enjoy observing the sky, apart from your eyes.

Although you will not be able to obtain close-up views of the Moon and planets, there is plenty more to see. It can be very helpful to get to know your way around the sky and learn how it changes before stepping up a gear and mastering a piece of optical equipment. Take time to learn the different star patterns, or constellations.

Start with the easy ones such as the Great Bear, or Orion, then use these as signposts to help locate other constellations nearby. The more you learn, the more quickly you will fill in the gaps to complete the celestial jigsaw. The human brain is good at making out patterns, and it will not be long before the stars appear not as random points of light scattered across the sky but as instantly recognizable shapes. You will note, as ancient man did, that they return to greet you at particular times of the year. Such familiarity was vital for our ancestors in helping them know when to plant crops, for example. For today's astronomer, it is a welcome connection with the natural rhythm of the calendar.

Learning the constellations is also a solid grounding for when you finally use a telescope and have to decide where in the sky to point it.

NAKED EYE ASTRONOMY

What sort of astronomy can you carry out with your eyes alone? You have taken your time and learned the star patterns, so where to look?

Comet Hale-Bopp over Stonehenge – you don't need a powerful telescope to witness incredible sights in the night sky.

As the sky darkens you can make key observations about the elementary effects of the Earth's rotation and journey around the Sun. Did you know that, on a perfectly clear day, you can look towards the opposite horizon and watch the Earth's own shadow rising in the sky? This appears as a red-tinged, deep mauve band that lifts slowly and expands across the sky as dusk deepens, bringing the natural darkness of night. Staying with sunsets – and sunrises – note how the position of these phenomena along the horizon varies depending on the time of year.

In northern latitudes, where midsummer occurs in June, the tilt of our axis in space means the Sun rises around the north-eastern point on the horizon, rises to a

"Learning the constellations is a good solid grounding that you will appreciate."

high point in the sky at local noon, then sets to the north-west. In midwinter, note how the Sun rises in the south-east, struggles to get very high in the sky at all, then slinks back below the horizon in the south-west. For southern hemisphere observers, of course, these midsummer and midwinter dates are reversed.

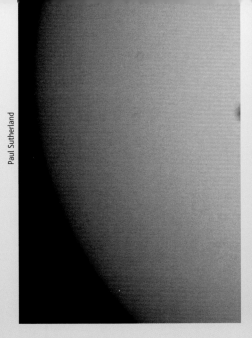

A naked eye sunspot.

The lunar seas of the moon can be seen with the naked eye as shown by this moonrise over Temple of Poseidon near Athens.

While the Sun is in the sky, you can check for naked eye sunspots: those darker regions of solar activity which occasionally become big enough to be seen with the eyes alone. Only attempt to look if you have a suitable filter, such as the special specs handed out for eclipse viewing (make sure they are completely undamaged), or a number-14 welder's glass.

Do NOT attempt to use old film negatives or underexposed slides as they are not safe and will not protect your eyes. If you do see a naked eye sunspot, then you can watch it from day to day and, if it survives long enough, note how the Sun is rotating on its axis.

As the sky darkens, watch the other celestial bodies appear. The Moon may already have been visible in the daytime sky, but it will become a lot more obvious as it shines against a darker backdrop. You will not be able to see any crater detail with just your eyes, but you could note the shapes of the lunar seas – the maria – and note brighter and darker regions.

If you catch the Moon shortly after First Quarter, you can actually see a lunar mountain range, the Apennines, curving down the dark terminator that divides the shadowed part of the moon from the side in sunlight.

After the Moon, the next objects to appear will be the brighter planets. If Mercury is at a favorable elongation, look for its star-like point low towards the horizon. Brilliant Venus will reveal itself first, being the third brightest object in the sky. Indeed, if you know just where to look and have very clear blue skies, Venus can be seen in broad daylight. It may take a while to locate but, once you have found it, you will wonder how you ever missed it.

A good way to achieve this is to use a planetarium program on your computer to note when the crescent Moon lies near Venus. Then find the Moon in the daytime sky and use it as a guide to your target. Try this only when Venus is further from the Sun, around the time of elongation, and obscure the Sun behind a building or tree so that its glare does not hinder you.

As the brighter stars start to show themselves, so too will the other bright planets – Jupiter, Saturn and Mars – assuming that they are above the horizon. Note their distinctive colors and see how their light appears steady. The stars twinkle, because they are distant pinpricks of light whose brightness is distorted by the atmosphere.

An interesting project is to note the slowly-changing position of the planets against the starry background. If you plot their paths, you will see how they stick close to the ecliptic, that imaginary line through the zodiac, and see how the superior planets appear to perform their little loops in the sky as the Earth overtakes them in its orbit each year. These are fun projects, which you can also produce

Paul Sutherland

"It might come as a suprise but, with practice, an observer may estimate a variable star's brightness, or magnitude, with considerable accuracy by comparing it to other stars of known brightness"

astronomical observations adding to scientific knowledge.

The meteor showers the Earth encounters every year are by no means predictable. Just by sitting for an hour or more assiduously watching a patch of sky, you can keep a log of the number of meteor streaks which appear. By tracing their paths backwards, you will learn to distinguish between those that are shower members and the so-called sporadics appearing any time and at random.

The more time and the more nights you are willing to spend meteor-watching, the more valuable your observations become. When combined with results from other observers around the world, such monitoring helps professional astronomers to learn about the distribution of dust through the solar system and the make-up of the meteors' parent comets. If you join a major astronomical society, it will give you advice and be happy to add your results to those of others.

Another science ideally suited to naked eye observers is following the changing brightness of variable stars. A number are bright enough to be seen without optical aid. Some, such as Cepheids or eclipsing binaries like Algol in Perseus, undergo changes which can be

forecast precisely. But others, notably the red giant stars, are far less predictable and tracking these provides useful data.

With practice an observer may estimate a variable star's brightness, or magnitude, with considerable accuracy by comparing it to other stars of known fixed brightness. Once again, combining one's observations with those of others add to the precision of the results.

As you watch the stars, you will sometimes spot a light moving slowly. This is more likely than not a satellite. Experience helps one distinguish these from aircraft, which usually show more than one light. Satellites high above us shine by reflected sunlight and can be seen slowly to fade as their orbits carry them into the Earth's shadow.

The big daddy of satellites is the International Space Station, which shines as a more and more brilliant star as astronauts add new sections to it. You can use the internet to be notified of times when the ISS passes over your location.

As well as these predictable phenomena, unexpected events occasionally occur which

The International Space Station is easy to spot with the naked eye. Here it fades as it flies into the Earth's shadow.

will interest the naked eye observer, such as the appearance of a particularly bright comet or possibly a nova exploding to brilliance deep in the galaxy. These rare events are further evidence that the sky is always changing.

BINOCULARS

A pair of binoculars greatly increases your observational range, since they are basically a compact pair of low-power telescopes offering a wide field of view. This makes them ideal for viewing star clusters and nebulae as well as the brighter comets. Even if you acquire a telescope, binoculars remain an invaluable item of equipment.

Pocket binoculars with smaller lenses collect a lot less light and are not recommended, except as a spare traveling pair. At the other end of the scale, are binoculars with 3.9in/100mm or 4.9in/125mm lenses and a magnification of 25-30 times. These expensive instruments are designed to be placed on solid mountings like telescopes and will be heavy and unwieldy without.

You may find it a strain to hold binoculars for long periods of time, especially while pointing them up at the sky. And, if you cannot hold your binoculars steady, it will be difficult to keep the objects you are observing in view. You can buy simple attachments which allow mounting binoculars on a photographer's tripod. If that is not possible, you may be able to support your elbows by observing from a garden chair or leaning against a wall.

Be careful not to drop your binoculars; heavy impact may dislodge the prisms which help fold the light path into a compact size. This will put the two barrels of the binoculars out of alignment and, even if it's by too slight an amount for you to notice, could cause headaches.

Binoculars are generally very reasonably priced. As always, be careful when purchasing: some are little more than toys while others, often advertised in newspapers, offer high, unrealistic magnifications making them almost impossible to use.

Binoculars are usually described in terms of their magnification and the diameter of their lenses in millimeters. So a pair of 10x50s, for example, have twin lenses, each 2in/50mm across, and a magnifying power of 10. A pair of that size will offer an ideal tool for scanning the night sky, producing wide views rich with stars. Another popular and useful size is 8x30. It's best not to pick much greater magnifying power, as they will also magnify shaking hand movements by the same degree.

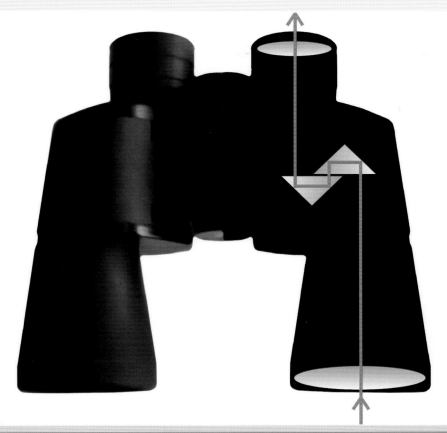

If you buy binoculars at a store, make sure you give them a basic checkover, and ask to look through them outside so that you can view a distant object. You can then at least tell if there is anything seriously wrong with their alignment. You may feel self-conscious doing this, but it's as useful as lying on a bed in a furniture store before purchase.

A recent and expensive development has been image-stabilizing binoculars. These work because they contain a special prism which instantly adjusts its alignment to counter the movements of your hands.

TOP: *A cutaway diagram shows how light passes through prisms in popular binoculars.*
ABOVE: *A typical view of the moon as seen through a pair of binoculars.*
LEFT: *Image-stabilizing binoculars are pricey but can compensate for shaking hands .*

TELESCOPES

Telescopes come in many shapes and sizes, but they all perform the same function: collecting radiation from space and magnifying it.

A medium-sized refracting telescope on an equatorial mount is ideal for viewing planets.

Optical telescopes collect light while other professional telescopes may collect signals from other parts of the rainbow-like electromagnetic spectrum – radio telescopes observe radio waves, for example.

The optical telescopes used by amateur astronomers come in various forms, but all work in the same way: by collecting more light from an object than the eye can manage alone, and focusing it so that it can be viewed.

In a simple refracting telescope, or refractor, the light-collecting part is a large lens called an objective. Its curved surfaces take parallel rays of light from an object and refract them along a tube towards the point where they converge. The distance of this point from the lens determines its focal length.

A second important element of the refractor is the eyepiece: a magnifying lens, or set of lenses, used to magnify the image produced by the main lens. Astronomers normally use a range of eyepieces to observe objects at different levels of magnification.

The second basic type of optical telescope is the Newtonian reflecting telescope, or reflector. Invented by Sir Isaac Newton, this instrument uses a curved mirror called the primary, a sophisticated version of the shaving mirror, which sits at the bottom of a tube and collects the light.

A 6in reflector is a useful and portable telescope. Here an observer peers through the finder to line up on a target.

Light rays are directed back up the tube to a much smaller, flat mirror, at a 45 degree angle, called the secondary. This directs the light out through a hole in the side of the tube, where the eyepiece is placed in its focusing mount.

The main mirror's curve is usually parabolic in shape, although smaller, cheaper models may be ground to a simpler spherical form.

Yoji Hirose

An 8in reflector is a useful size for observing galaxies, clusters and planets. Reflecting telescopes avoid false color problems but can slip out of alignment more easily than refractors.

more detail to view on their favored targets. Amateurs who prefer to observe star clusters, galaxies and nebulae often choose the shorter focal lengths, because the instruments let them view wider areas of the sky with brighter stars and other objects. These instruments are often termed Rich-Field Telescopes, or RFTs.

Both these two main types of telescope have their fans. Refractors are especially convenient as smaller, portable telescopes. The smallest useful size is usually considered to have an objective lens 60mm in diameter. Reflectors are cheaper to build when it comes to larger instruments, and some amateurs are today working with mirrors 20in or more in diameter, although 6in-8in is a much more common size.

Refractors suffer an effect where light passing through the objective gets refracted to slightly different points, depending on its color. This is called chromatic aberration and leads to objects being observed showing colorful fringes around them. Telescope manufacturers attempt to counter this failing by using a combination of lenses, rather than one alone, to form the objective. The most successful, and expensive, are called apochromatic refractors, which show little, if any, signs of fringes.

With either a refracting telescope or a reflector, the greater the size of your objective or primary mirror, the more light you will receive from the object you are observing and, generally speaking, the more you will be able to magnify it. Dividing the focal length of the telescope by the diameter of the objective or mirror will tell you the telescope's focal ratio. You can combine this with the focal length of the eyepiece to work out the power of magnification needed.

The greater the curve of the lens or mirror, the shorter the focal length and the smaller the focal ratio. Planetary observers look for long focal lengths because it gives them

There are other types of optical telescope marrying the two basic forms, and they're becoming increasingly popular with amateur astronomers. Termed catadioptric telescopes, they combine mirrors and lenses to produce a compact instrument with a long focal length. The main mirrors are spherical and so easier to manufacture, and a glass corrector plate at the top of the tube compensates for any distortions this would normally introduce. The telescope's secondary mirror then sends the light back towards a hole in the center of the main mirror, beyond which the eyepiece is placed. The most common sort of catadioptric telescope is the Schmidt-Cassegrain. Others include the Maksutov and Ritchey-Chrétien. One point which distinguishes an astronomical telescope, and which you will notice at once if you look at Earth-bound objects, is that it turns them upside down. This so-called inverted image is accepted by astronomers. Terrestrial telescopes have another lens attachment added to turn things the right way up, but this extra bit would cut down some of that vital light from the heavens.

Similarly, some catadioptric telescopes, such as in Meade's ETX range, give a mirror image of objects, because their light is reflected three times during its passage through the compact optical arrangement.

Paul Sutherland

ABOVE: *Amateur astronomer Martin Lewis at a UK star party with the giant 20in reflecting telescope he built himself. Monster instruments like this offer superb views of galaxies and nebulae although portability is sacrificed.*

LEFT: *Meade's ETX range provides a popular choice of small catadioptric telescopes that are are portable and have built-in computer controls.*

HOW TO CHOOSE A TELESCOPE

There has probably never been a better time to buy a telescope, since they are less expensive in real terms than they have ever been. Much of this is due to the scale of manufacture as well as construction techniques at the factories, which are often found in the Far East, particularly China. You can pay a reasonable sum, perhaps similar to the cost of a simple digital camera, and obtain an extremely useful instrument.

> "It's important to pick a telescope that suits your own circumstances. If you live in acity apartment and need to drive out of town to stargaze, choose a portable telescope"

The important factors are that the optics are of good quality and the telescope sits on a firm mounting, because magnification you apply to an image will also magnify vibrations by a similar amount. Beware of many cheap toy telescopes, such as those found in catalogs, which may have poor lenses and flimsy support. Auction sites on the internet are also home to some rather dubious lesser-known brands.

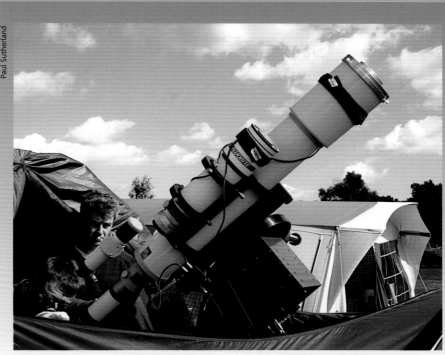

Paul Sutherland

Astronomers with deep pockets pay large sums for top-of-the range refracting telescopes with high-quality optics. This set-up is sheltered in a purpose-designed observing tent.

It's also important to pick a telescope that suits your circumstances. If you live in a city apartment and need to drive out of town stargaze, you will need one which is portable and can be set up and dismantled swiftly and easily. If you have a country home with room for a permanent observatory, you will be able to consider a larger and heavier instrument.

Seek advice from other, experienced amateurs. If you join a local astronomical group grab the chance to look through other members' telescopes and find the one that suits you best. Many groups organize observing sessions or star parties, where you can check out an array of instruments. Although the entry prices for telescopes is generally reasonable, it is still as true in amateur astronomy, as in other areas of life, that you get what you pay for. For the highest-quality telescopes with particularly fine optics, metal tubes and other parts, plus a really solid mounting, you will be asked to part with a lot more money.

Another important point with cheaper telescopes is that the manufacturers often save on costs by providing two or three very basic eyepieces. It's generally well worth investing in at least two or three good quality eyepieces straight away. You can buy these without breaking the bank, the improvement in telescope performance will be huge.

EYEPIECES
AND OTHER ACCESSORIES

The most important accessory for your telescope is the eyepiece. With your telescope, you may have already received two or three, to give you different powers of magnification.

If you have one of the cheaper telescopes, your eyepieces will probably contain simple lenses. Better quality eyepieces, which you should consider buying, consist of a more sophisticated arrangement of higher grade lenses arranged in a metal tube called a barrel. They are made to standard diameters, with basic models having a barrel diameter of 1.25in, so you can switch from your cheap eyepieces to quality optics without much fuss. Serious amateurs often adapt their telescopes to use eyepieces 2in in diameter.

Eyepieces are available in a number of different forms, depending on their physical design. These include the kellner, the orthoscopic, the ramsden and the erfle. But the industry today seems to have settled on one design, called the plossl, for most telescopes made for amateur astronomers.

Whereas telescopes are usually described by the diameter of their primary lens or mirror, eyepieces get described by their focal lengths – 0.4in/10mm, 0.8in/20mm and so on. These will magnify by different amounts, depending on the telescope.

Divide the focal length of the telescope by the focal length of the eyepiece, making sure you use the same units in each case. So if you have a refractor with a focal length of 19in/480mm and you insert a 0.8in/20mm eyepiece, your magnification will be 24 times. Switch to a 0.35in/9mm eyepiece and the magnification becomes 53 times.

You can find eyepieces with much shorter focal lengths, but there will be practical limits, depending on the size of your telescope and therefore its light-collecting ability, as well as the steadiness of the atmosphere on any particular night.

Eyepieces come in many different types, shapes and sizes, and their designs offer different magnifications and apparent fields of view. A barlow lens, like that pictured on the left, can be placed between an eyepiece and telescope to increase the power of magnification.

"A star diagonal saves you from having to stoop and squint through the tube of a refractor for an object high in the sky."

at a 90 degree angle. It can make observing an object high in the sky much more comfortable when using a refractor, because it saves you having to stoop down and squint up the tube. The barlow lens and star diagonal with cheaper telescopes are likely to be of very basic quality, and you may want to upgrade.

The finderscope or finder is a smaller and simple telescope attached to the side of the main tube which helps line up on a celestial object. These can be tricky to use, and it's wise to ensure that yours is aligned correctly with the telescope by testing on, say, a distant chimney pot or radio mast during daylight. Get that in the center of a high-power eyepiece, clamp the telescope so that it cannot wander, then adjust the finder screws to make sure the object lies in the center of its field of view as well.

An increasing trend is for finderscopes to be replaced by a red dot finder that uses an LED to project a virtual bright dot, which is pointed at the target.

If atmospheric currents are making Jupiter wobble, it will be better to observe with a lower power eyepiece. On rare nights of still air, when the planet barely ripples, you can switch to higher powers.

The telescope may also arrive with something else resembling an eyepiece, called a barlow lens. This device increases the magnification of any eyepiece that is inserted into it, usually by two times. It can therefore double the capabilities of your entire collection of eyepieces.

A wedge-shaped item in the telescope package is likely to be a star diagonal, into which eyepieces are inserted. This holds a prism directing the light passing through a telescope

If you are starting out, invest in a special eyepiece and filter kit that comes already cased. The range of eyepieces will suit many observing situations and the filters, though not essential, will help bring out colors or add contrast when you are viewing nebulae or observing detail.

MOUNTINGS

When choosing a telescope, don't neglect the mounting. Its quality is as important as any other part of the instrument.

A small refracting telescope on a simple alt-azimuth mount which would make an appropriate starter instrument for a child.

Superb optics are of little use if they are supported by a rickety mount which vibrates at the slightest touch. Those vibrations will magnify greatly and ruin attempts to observe when you look through the scope.

A shop-bought telescope usually comes with a tripod, which may be made of aluminum or wood. At the top of the tripod is the mount. There are two basic types – the alt-azimuth and the equatorial mounts – although you will find them in various forms.

Alt-azimuth mounts are the simplest and will swivel the telescope in two directions: up and down in altitude – the alt bit – and around

parallel to the horizon – the azimuth. This is a perfectly adequate way of using a telescope for terrestrial viewing and for simple star spotting. But after just a few moments of astronomical use, you will discover the limitations.

Earlier in the book, we described the basic geometry of the celestial sphere and how the sky appears to turn as the Earth rotates. From most parts of the globe, any astronomical body will seem to drift in both altitude and azimuth during this process. This means that you will have to keep moving your telescope sideways and up or down simultaneously to keep it in your field of view. The only exceptions are if you live on the Equator, where you will simply have to move the scope vertically, or at the north or south pole, where you will only need to swing it horizontally.

All alt-azimuth mounts, whatever the designs, will perform in the same fashion. You might find one atop a tripod supporting a cheap refractor. A different type turns the popular Dobsonian reflecting telescope, where the rotating parts are close to the ground.

Many modern 'goto' telescopes come with an alt-azimuth mount but the built-in computer adjusts both elevation and azimuth constantly

to keep the instrument on target.

Equatorial mounts were designed to make astronomers' lives easier, although they can seem a difficult concept to grasp for a beginner. The central shaft, or polar axis, of the mounting is angled to point towards the north or south celestial pole, so that it is aligned with the Earth's own axis. This allows the telescope again to be moved in two directions, but instead of those being

Meade's computerized LX200 range of telescopes uses fork mounts which can be set up in alt-azimuth or equatorial mode.

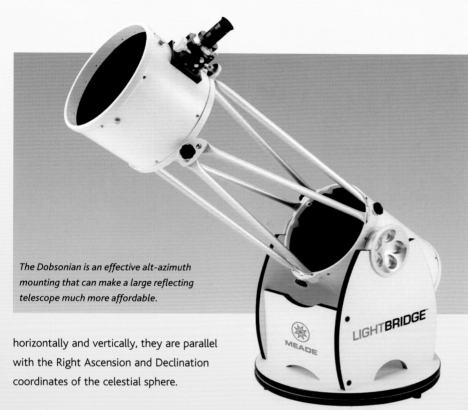

The Dobsonian is an effective alt-azimuth mounting that can make a large reflecting telescope much more affordable.

A popular form of the equatorial mount is the German mounting, on which the telescope tube is held to one side of the polar axis, on the end of the declination axis. This requires a suitable counterweight to be placed on the other side of the declination axis to maintain balance.

Another form of equatorial mount has the optical telescope sitting in a fork-type mounting on top of the polar axis. This is commonly used to mount giant professional telescopes, although Meade's ETX is held in the same way when set up equatorially.

horizontally and vertically, they are parallel with the Right Ascension and Declination coordinates of the celestial sphere.

The beauty of the equatorial mount is that, once the telescope is pointed at a star or planet, it will then only have to be turned on one axis to follow that object as the Earth rotates. An electric motor drive may be fitted to turn the telescope automatically, and nowadays this often uses a computerized system.

For the system to work, it is essential that the mount is aligned correctly in the first place.

If you live in the northern hemisphere, you will first need to place your tripod mount so that it stands level and the polar axis is lined up in the direction of north on the horizon. A clamp will allow you to alter the angle at which the shaft points upwards. Make sure that this angle corresponds with the latitude of your own location. In London, for example, the polar axis should be turned to an angle of

51 degrees. In New York, this angle should be 41 degrees.

With the aid of a compass, you should be able to set up your mounting in this way in daylight and it will serve you well for casual viewing. For even more precise orientation, more expensive mounts contain a mini-telescope within the polar axis, so that you can make sure that Polaris, the star that lies close to the north celestial pole, is properly positioned.

In the southern hemisphere, the procedure is very similar except that you should align your mount's polar axis in a southerly direction and then adjust its angle to your own latitude south of the equator. It should be 34 degrees, for example, for an astronomer living in Sydney, Australia.

Paul Sullivan

A small, computer-controlled telescope from Celestron, fitted with a solar filter. Despite an alt-azimuth set-up, the computer will easily find and follow objects observed.

GETTING READY

A golden rule when planning an observing session is: make sure you are comfortable. Observing in shirt-sleeves may be possible in some lucky parts of the world, but in many others nights can feel very cold indeed, even after a warm, sunny day.

It is important to wear suitable clothes.

Some of the gear that an amateur might use to observe and take notes. Fingerless mittens make them easier to handle.

The most spectacular comet in the sky can seem a lot less appealing if you are wearing just a thin top and the temperature is below zero. Any strong breeze will make it seem colder than usual, due to what weathermen call the wind-chill factor. It may seem obvious, but try to find an observing spot that is sheltered from the wind.

So make sure you are well wrapped up, preferably in several layers to help trap the air, and with a wind-resistant outer coat. A woolly hat is important as considerable body heat is lost from the head. Choose thick socks and good boots to keep your feet warm. It can help if you stand on a mat to help insulate yourself further against the cold ground. You will probably need a pair of warm gloves too, and fingerless mittens can be very useful if you are taking notes or operating fiddly controls on your telescope.

Skiwear is ideal, even if you are not going anywhere near any mountains or snow. Mainstream stores now offer outfits at reasonable prices, and often discounts on last year's fashions.

A deckchair will make life easier for binocular users sweeping the heavens for clusters and nebulae, particularly if it has arms on which to rest your elbows. It also makes life a lot more comfortable if you are simply observing with your eyes. Being able to lean back in a relaxed position will also help you to avoid getting a cricked neck. Another option for binocular observers is to place the instrument on a tripod. Remember to take a few snacks and a hot drink with you if you are going to be viewing for long periods of time.

If you are using a telescope, make sure it is positioned so that you can view through it comfortably. You might be able to extend the legs of the tripod, for example, or sit on a stool to look through the eyepiece more comfortably.

But however cold it is, try not to be tempted to take your telescope indoors to observe. If you point your instrument through a window to view your target, the warmth of the house will create air currents that will distort the image and make proper observing impossible, especially at higher magnifications.

Observing is not much fun if you drop something vital, like a screw, and then have to scrabble around to find it in the darkness. One solution is to put down a groundsheet or blanket before setting up your telescope, so that it catches anything that falls.

PROBLEMS THAT OBSERVERS FACE

Astronomy comes with its disappointments. Many a night you will find your observing plans thwarted by bad weather, or an eclipse of the Sun can be obsured by clouds.

The vagaries of the climate are a major problem for astronomers and, to be honest, there's not a lot that one can do about it aside from getting to know how weather patterns work.

Neither can we do much about the fact that the Moon, at its brightest phases, will conspire to drown out many of the fainter and more delicate sights we might want to see.

The trick is to plan your observing sessions to take account of the best times to see the best sights. Reserve nights around New Moon for hunting out deep sky targets and then use the moonlit nights to study the fascinating features found on our natural satellite.

Another enemy of the astronomer is light pollution. Everyone is keen to be environment-minded these days, but we continue to drown out the wonders of the sky in a luminous fog. Even with improvements in streetlight design, too much wasted light is spread into the heavens. The situation is often exacerbated by the proliferation of domestic security lighting pointing upwards to the skies.

A century ago, people could step outside their homes and stare up at a dark sky studded with stars. Today, in many parts of the world, they will see nothing but an orange haze.

There are organizations battling to reverse o at least control the damage, but we have a long way to go before we can t look out anc appreciate our place in the universe.

Even a sparse amount of cloud cover can spoil your view.

The lamp on the left will shine light directly downwards, replacing the old lamp that spreads light in all directions.

The long white trail running through the center is a space station that has been captured as it heads towards orbit. Light pollution has made this bright orbiting outpost harder to see.

Clouds rolling in as evening approaches can mean disappointment and a wasted night for an astronomer.

In many heavily populated regions of the world, we have to travel away from home to enjoy an interest in astronomy. Always be aware of your personal safety and be careful, also, not to trespass.

Observing is not much fun if you find a nice country spot only to be bothered by strange animal noises, a worried farmer, courting couples or a police patrol. There's nothing like headlights on full beam to ruin a session observing faint galaxies.

Astronomy is often a solitary pursuit but you might feel a lot more comfortable sharing a remote observing session with a fellow enthusiast.

Even if the sky is cloud-free, the weather can still affect observation. You will want to make sure you are sheltered if a strong wind is blowing, and certain times of year can bring the curse of the night: humidity.

When telescopes cool in humid air, they quickly collect dew, producing a film of water across the optics and making observing very difficult.

Amateur astronomers counter this in various ways. Extend the length of your telescope's dew cap, or create one, by wrapping a sheet of black paper, plastic or foam into a cylinder around the front end of the tube. How about taking the telescope into a shed or outhouse for a short while now and again, to allow it to warm up?

You can buy special anti-dew heaters which coil around the telescope's objective lens to warm it up and prevent dew from forming. Some people use portable hair-dryers to give the optics a quick blast and clear them every now and again.

Nights that appear to be clear can still provide very different viewing conditions, and what may seem a wonderful frosty night with sparkling stars may be a disappointment through the telescope. On such nights, a planet might seem to jump around and show little detail, because the atmosphere is unstable. On other exceptional nights, all may seem particularly calm with the planets steady and revealing more. Astronomers describe these changing conditions as "the seeing".

Incidentally, you may notice nights when the stars twinkle but planets don't. This is because we see even the closest stars to us as just points of light. The planets are tiny disks, even if they are not obvious to the naked eye, and so the distortion by the atmosphere is less spectacular.

SKETCHING AND RECORDING

Don't expect to be able to observe the intricacies of the sky immediately. The eyes are remarkably efficient at adapting to a wide range of brightnesses, but it takes time for them to adapt.

You will have noticed a similar effect when you go from the light into a dark room. You see nothing at first, but as your eyes adjust and pupils grow larger, you are able to make out objects.

When you step out beneath a dark sky, your eyes will take several minutes to be at their most sensitive and become, as astronomers say, "dark adapted". So go for the brighter targets in the sky first, before you attempt to hunt out a faint object such as a nebula. Avoid white lights while you are observing, which might mean closing your eyes or looking away if car headlights suddenly appear.

Fortunately, the eyes are a lot less sensitive to red light, so you can check out star charts or an observing guide by using a torch covered with red film or with red LEDs.

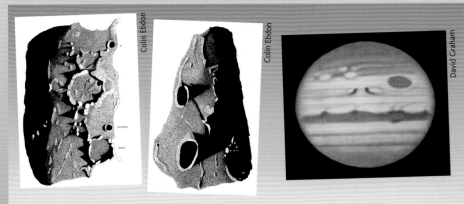

Despite the popularity of imaging equipment, it is still rewarding to make your own sketches, such as those here of lunar craters Guericke, left, Diophantus and Delisle, and planet Jupiter.

Use a red light so you don't ruin your "dark adapted" vision.

When you are at the telescope, even if you are dark adapted and the seeing is ideal, you should not expect to see all there is in an object straight away. A cursory glance at Saturn, for example, will show the ball of the planet and its rings, but it takes time and experience to discern the subtle shadings in the image.

In an age when we expect instant gratification, it can be immensely rewarding to take the time and patience to look at an object carefully. It's doubly rewarding if you keep notes or make sketches of what you are observing. You don't need to be a great

artist; just some simple shadings can give an indication of what you saw. The result will be that, in time, you build up a fascinating observing log – something to enjoy looking through on those cloudy nights years later.

When you have gained experience in drawing the planets, the Moon's craters, or a nebula or galaxy in deep space, you may find that your observations will be welcomed by of the larger astronomical societies collecting records of members' work. Many supply special template forms, called blanks, for you to sketch on. Observers usually make a rough sketch of a planet at the eyepiece and then make a copy

on such a form for sending to the society.

It is quite normal, by the way, to sketch, say, a nebula in a negative way, with the brightest areas shown darkest and the dark sky left white. The human brain is able to invert an image in this way.

Similar template forms are provided for written observations of other celestial events, such as meteor showers or variable stars. The work amateurs do in these areas provides a valuable service to professional astronomers researching these phenomena.

If you're observing meteors, amateur organizations are keen that contributors keep watch on nights other than those of predicted maximum activity, and even on nights when there are no known showers and only the sporadics on view. This way we learn more about the level of meteor activity throughout the year.

If you are monitoring variable stars, be careful not to allow bias to affect your work. Be ready for anything, and report what you actually see. Just because a star has been brightening and might be expected to be brighter still when you are looking, does not mean that it really will be. Try to keep an open mind.

An example of one of the templates provided by larger astronomical societies.

Specialist groups provide charts to help locate and estimate the brightness of variable stars.

PHOTOGRAPHING THE SKY

Photography is an excellent way to record astronomical events. Astrophotography is an increasingly popular method, though we are usually working with much lower levels of light than we have in daytime photography.

You will often want to experiment with different exposures and other settings, if that is possible with your camera, to obtain decent results. The great advantage of modern digital cameras is that you can see straight away whether you have been successful and adjust accordingly.

If you have a basic camera and have to take a quick snapshot of the night sky, the chances are that little, if anything, will show. You will be limited to twilight landscape shots with perhaps a crescent Moon or Venus in the picture. To record anything more of the stars, your camera will need to be capable of taking time exposures. This ability is built into single lens reflex (SLR) cameras, whether film or digital, where it may be shown as the Bulb, or B, setting.

The Bulb setting enables you to open the shutter and release it after a chosen amount of time has elapsed. Place your camera on a tripod and use a cable release to take the exposure to produce images that do not show camera shake. Better digital SLRs allow you to control the exposure with a cable directly from your computer. Remember to turn off the flash.

Cameras allow you to set an exposure of several seconds. If you have no cable release, use this setting, together with the shutter delay that is usually intended to allow photographers to become the subjects of their own pictures. This workaround will avoid the shake introduced by pressing the shutter button with your finger.

It will only require a very few seconds of exposure before a surprising number of stars record on your image. If you are using a standard lens and your exposure lasts longer than 15 to 20 seconds, you will notice that the stars appear stretched. They are beginning to show trailing, the effect of the rotation of the Earth.

A time-exposure of a few minutes will be enough for stars to trail in your photograph as the Earth rotates.

"It will only require a few seconds of exposure before a surprising number of stars record on your image"

The way to avoid this effect in longer time exposures is to mount your camera on a guided platform that counteracts the Earth's rotation. You could mount it piggyback on a telescope with a motor drive, for example – but it will need to be properly aligned.

You will find practical limits in the exposures that you take, such as the amount of light pollution that will build up in your image, and the electronic "noise" that may build up in a digital camera. But your shots could indicate, for example, how, they stars circle the celestial poles in little arcs, the stars' paths are longer and straighter around the celestial equator. If you are using film, you may find that the stars' colors show clearly in your exposures. Unfortunately, digital cameras seem less capable of recording star color in such shots.

The sensitivity of different types of film to light used to be measured by its ISO rating, such as 100 ISO, 200 ISO, 400 ISO. This determines the speed of the film, the higher numbers being faster. The system is still used following the arrival of digital

Paul Sutherland

This shot of the Moon was taken with a snapshot camera attached to the eyepiece of a small telescope.

photography, although everything is handled electronically.

Faster settings are very effective at capturing fainter stars, but the longer the exposure, the greater the risk that light pollution will build up. Digital cameras may suffer the additional problem of electronic noise, which shows itself as bright dots or patches in your

pictures. Noise reduction systems are usually built in, with varying degrees of success. It's worth experimenting with different exposure times and ISO speeds to test the results.

Obviously, the major benefit of digital imaging is that you can import your photos directly into a computer for processing and enhancing. For greatest flexibility during processing, take your images at the camera's RAW setting, if it has one, although you need the relevant software that can handle this format.

Long exposures with digital cameras, or electronic film cameras can run down camera batteries, so make sure you carry a spare. They don't last so long in cold conditions. This is an area where the old mechanical SLR cameras come into their own.

If you have a telescope, you could hold the camera to a focused eyepiece and fire a few shots of the Moon. Its surface brightness is comparable to snapping a landscape view on Earth, so your camera may well give you a pleasing result. Some amateurs, just for fun, have even tried such snaps with the cameras built into mobile phones, with recognizable results!

The difficulty with using this "afocal" approach is lining up the camera and eyepiece correctly. If the camera is only slightly tilted,

This superb picture of Saturn was taken using a CCD camera, then enhanced

the Moon's image will miss the film or chip in the camera. You could mount your camera on a tripod alongside the telescope to help, although you would need to keep moving the set-up as the Moon drifts out of view due to the rotation of the Earth. Another option is to purchase adaptors which allow you to clamp the camera over the eyepiece, or even join the two together.

You may get simple snaps of the brighter planets in this way. Just don't expect much in the way of detail.

The same techniques may be used with video cameras, although attaching any heavy device to the telescope can cause problems balancing the instrument's weight.

If you have an SLR camera, you may be able to remove the lens from your camera and then attach the telescope without its eyepiece, so it effectively becomes a telephoto lens. This is called prime focus photography and usually requires a simple adapter for the telescope, plus a T-mount specific to your camera model.

A lucky gift for astrophotography was the appearance of the webcam in computing.

Camera adaptors (T-mounts)

The device's sensitivity to low light makes it useful for recording images of the Moon and planets through the telescope. It's also light enough to be attached without the balancing problems introduced by normal cameras. You can buy adapters that screw into the front of the webcam and allow it to sit in the eyepiece holder.

More sophisticated CCD cameras are produced specially for astronomy. These contain a charge-coupled device, which is a chip with an array of sensors that are highly receptive to the levels of light involved. The chips are generally cooled to reduce vastly any noise on the image from the electronics.

Images taken with webcams and their more sophisticated (and costly) CCD cousins can be processed with computers, to produce extraordinary results.

Eclipses can be fun to photograph. For solar eclipses, you will need the same sort of filters as you would use for viewing, otherwise you will quickly damage or destroy your camera. Lunar eclipses are a safe target but require a range of different exposures, depending on whether you are bringing out the part of the Moon still in sunlight or the region that is in shadow.

These are individual frames from a webcam "movie" through a small telescope. Best frames were selected and stacked to form a final image.

A final enhanced webcam image of Saturn.

COMPUTERS

Computers have made a major impact on every walk of life, and astronomy is no exception. Professional scientists use them extensively to process and analyze data, and to control telescopes that may be far away.

Computers ease researchers' work greatly when they are studying such things as how stars or planets form. The most complex space missions to distant planets and their moons are made possible by the power of the processor.

Not to be outdone, amateur astronomers have also taken up the challenge of computing. Their telescopes are now often driven by microprocessors with databases of stellar delights that tell them where to point. But they are also, like the professionals, using their home computers to work with the data that their observations have supplied.

Digital photographs, as described in the previous section, can be transformed into high-quality images thanks to computer techniques. Many amateurs are taking webcam "movies" of planets through their telescopes.

From possibly hundreds of individual frames, the sharpest, caught during moments of excellent seeing, are selected and the rest rejected. Special software then allows the good frames to be combined, or stacked. Finally, the image that is left is enhanced using the tools within photo-editing software. The results from amateurs using such techniques can be little short of stunning.

This is cutting-edge astronomy for dedicated amateurs, but computers are helping stargazing beginners, too, with a variety of programs that allow you to produce a planetarium on your desktop. These can accurately recreate the sky for any date and time and from any location on Earth. The best programs have the capability of showing beginners a realistic view of the night sky yet may be used by advanced amateurs to obtain precise details of astronomical events, and even to control their telescopes.

One of the most realistic planetarium programs is the free and remarkable Stellarium, which is available for PCs and Macs. It was used to help create the star maps in this book.

Of course, the internet has become a valuable resource for professional and amateur scientists alike. From our homes, we have access to all manner of databases and

Stellarium is an amazing piece of free software which creates a realistic view of the sky on your own home computer.

"From our homes, we have access to all manner of databases and information sources, including those provided by major observatories"

Celestron's SkyScout is a "point and shoot" tool using GPS to identify objects in the sky.

information sources, including those provided by major observatories and space agencies such as NASA. Some services are interactive and will produce anything from a star chart for your location to predictions of times and directions to find satellites such as the International Space Station when it passes over your part of the world. Others will simply provide galleries of images from telescopes and space probes that you can spend happy hours studying.

The internet has also aided communication between astronomers. Such social networking, to use the buzz phrase, ranges from the simple blogs that act like online observing logs to busy discussion forums and chatrooms where stargazers gather to talk about the latest events and seek advice.

The world's leading astronomical societies have extended their operations into cyberspace with useful websites to help keep members informed and assisted. Some astronomical websites offer reviews of telescopes, while others act to support users of particular models.

Or, of course, you can find and buy from dealers online or scour auction sites such as for a bargain. Reference resources such as online encyclopedias can bring you bang up to date on any aspect of science, and you can sign up to email bulletins that will notify you of the latest events in astronomy or space research.

GLOSSARY

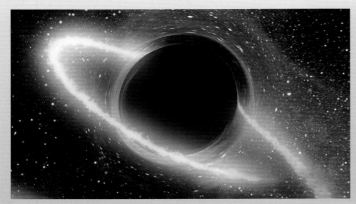

A black hole.

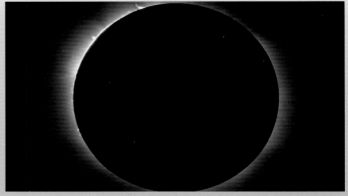

A total solar eclipse.

ABSOLUTE MAGNITUDE
The brightness at which a star would appear at a distance of ten parsecs (32.6 light-years) from the Earth, It allowing stellar brightnesses to be compared.

ACCRETION
The collecting together of dust and debris to form stars and planets.

ALBEDO
A term to describe the reflectivity of a planetary surface.

APHELION
A planet's furthest point from the Sun in its orbit. Earth reaches this in July.

APOGEE
The furthest point in the orbit of the Moon or a satellite around the Earth.

ARC MINUTE
An angular measure of separation between two points in the sky; one sixtieth of a degree. An arc second is one sixtieth of an arc minute.

ASTERISM
A small but distinct pattern of stars within a constellation.

ASTRONOMICAL UNIT
The average distance between the Earth and the Sun: equivalent to 93 million miles/ 149,597,870 km..

BINARY STAR
A pair of stars revolving around a common center of mass.

BLACK HOLE
An object with a gravitational field so powerful that no light or radiation within it can escape. Anything inside the black hole's event horizon is effectively cut off from the rest of the universe.

CELESTIAL EQUATOR
An imaginary line running around the celestial sphere directly above the Earth's equator.

CHROMATIC ABERRATION
False coloring seen in cheap refracting telescopes, due to simple lenses bringing different parts of the spectrum to focus at different points.

CHROMOSPHERE
The region of the Sun between the visible surface, or photosphere, and its corona.

CONJUNCTION
A close encounter in the sky between two bodies such as planets. It also describes the point when the outer planets pass on the far side of the Sun.

CONSTELLATION
Imaginary patterns of stars in the sky, originally created by ancient man. Today there are 88 official groupings, each with defined borders.

CORONA
The outer layer of the solar atmosphere, and its hottest part.

CULMINATION
The moment when a star or other object reaches its highest point in the sky during the daily turning of the heavens.

DECLINATION
A co-ordinate on the celestial sphere corresponding to latitude on the Earth. It is used along with Right Ascension to describe an object's position in the sky.

ECCENTRICITY
A description of how much an elliptical orbit is stretched from circular.

ECLIPSE
The term correctly applies when a body such as a moon or satellite moves into the shadow of another body. However, it is also used to describe the passage of the Moon in front of the Sun.

ECLIPTIC
The path that the Sun appears to take against the celestial sphere as the Earth orbits it each year.

ELONGATION
The apparent distance of an astronomical object from the Sun in the sky. Greatest elongation is used to describe the point when Mercury and Venus appear furthest from the Sun.

EQUATORIAL MOUNT
A telescope mount that allows the instrument to rotate in alignment with the celestial sphere. It counters the Earth's rotation and makes it easier to follow objects as they

A spiral galaxy.

Stars in the filaments of a nebula.

move across the sky.

EQUINOX
The date in March or September when the Earth's orbit makes the Sun appear to cross the Celestial Equator.

GALAXY
Vast 'cosmic cities' of many billions of stars held together by gravitational force.

GLOBULAR CLUSTER
A roughly spherical collection of older stars. They are often found in haloes around galaxies.

GRANULATION
The crystallized appearance of the visible surface of the Sun, caused by convection currents.

INCLINATION
The amount by which the plane of a planet or comet's orbit is tilted to the ecliptic.

INFERIOR PLANETS
Planets that lie inside the orbit of the Earth and are therefore closer to the Sun. They are Mercury and Venus.

KUIPER BELT
The region beyond Neptune where many thousands of icy, comet-like bodies are believed to lurk. Pluto is now thought to be part of this belt.

LIGHT YEAR
The distance that light travels in a year. The speed of light in a vacuum is 983,571,056ft/ 299,792,458m per second.

LUNATION
The length of time between one New Moon and the next.

MAGNETOSPHERE
A natural magnetic force field around a planet such as Earth that protects it from the solar wind.

MAGNITUDE
The scale by which stars' brightnesses are measured: the bigger the number, the fainter the star. Apparent magnitude describes how bright the stars appear. Bright stars such as Capella and Vega are zero magnitude. The faintest stars visible with the unaided eye in ideal conditions are around magnitude six. Absolute magnitude is the brightness they would show if all were placed at the same distance.

METEOR
The streak of light seen in the sky as a particle of debris vaporizes in the atmosphere. The particle itself, usually no bigger than a grain of sand, is called a meteoroid. Larger rocks that reach the ground are called meteorites.

NEBULA
A cloud of gas and dust. A nebula may shine by reflecting starlight or by being excited by stars within it, or it may be dark and reveal itself by blotting out stars further away.

NOCTILUCENT CLOUDS
Shimmering midnight clouds high in the atmosphere, seen particularly in summer months. Also known as mesospheric clouds.

OCCULTATION
The passage of one celestial body in front of another, such as the Moon in front of a star or planet. An eclipse of the Sun should properly be termed an occultation.

OPEN CLUSTER
A related collection of stars, randomly scattered.

OPPOSITION
The point when one of the outer planets is opposite the Sun in the sky.

ORBIT
The path one body, such as a planet or moon, takes around another with which it is gravitationally linked.

PARALLAX
The angular shift against the starry background that a closer object shows when viewed from two widely separated points, for example, opposite sides of the Earth's orbit.

PARSEC
A unit of measurement, equal to 3.2616 light years, used to describe huge distances in space.

PENUMBRA
The lighter outer shadow through which the Moon travels during a lunar eclipse. The term also describes the lighter surroundings of a dark sunspot.

PERIGEE
The closest point in the Moon's or a satellite's orbit around the Earth.

GLOSSARY

A planetary nebula.

A bright aurora.

PERIHELION
The point at which an orbiting planet or comet is closest to the Sun. The Earth is at perihelion in January.

PHOTOSPHERE
The Sun's visible surface on which sunspots are often seen.

PLANETARY NEBULA
A shell of gas ejected by a dying red giant star. It has nothing to do with planets and was so called because its shape resembled a planetary disk.

PRECESSION
A slow circular wobble of the Earth's axis over a period of 27,700 years. It means that Polaris, which roughly marks the position of the north celestial pole, is only temporarily the "pole star".

PROMINENCE
An ejection of hot gas into the Sun's corona. Special solar telescopes show them leaping from the edge of the Sun into space.

PULSAR
A rapidly spinning, collapsed neutron star left by a supernova. Pulsars can rotate hundreds of times a second, emitting radio signals so regular that it was briefly thought they might be from aliens when they first were discovered in 1967.

QUASAR
A highly luminous object at a vast distance, thought to be the active nucleus of a galaxy around a supermassive black hole. Short for Quasi-stellar radio source.

RADIANT
The point in the sky from which meteors in a meteor shower appear to come. It is purely an effect of perspective because the meteoroids are traveling in parallel paths. Meteor showers are usually named after the constellation in which the radiant lies.

RED SHIFT
An effect that causes the signature lines marking the elements in a spectrum to shift towards the red in light from an object moving away from the observer at great speed.

RIGHT ASCENSION (RA)
The co-ordinates on the celestial sphere that correspond to lines of longitude on the Earth. The 24 hours of RA equate to 360 degrees. RA, together with an object's Declination, will pinpoint an object's position against the sky.

SIDEREAL TIME
Time measured by the stars rather than the Sun. The Sidereal Day is 23h 56m long.

SOLAR CYCLE
An 11-year variation in activity on the Sun.

SOLSTICE
The points in June and December when the Sun reaches its most northerly or southerly position in the sky.

SUPERNOVA
A star that destroys itself in a catastrophic explosion.

TERMINATOR
The boundary between the day side and night side of a planet or moon.

UMBRA
The main dark shadow in a lunar eclipse or the central region of a sunspot.

VARIABLE STAR
A star whose brightness changes over time.

ZENITH
The point in the sky that lies directly overhead.

ZODIAC
Loved by astrologers, this is the band of sky through which the Sun and planets appear to travel.

ZODIACAL LIGHT
A ghostly glow caused by sunlight reflecting off particles of interplanetary dust.